"PURPLE MOUNTAIN MAJESTIES ABOVE THE FRUITED PLAIN"

WORLD OVER STORIES

For Junior Boys and Girls

FLOYD W. LAMBERTSON

THE ABINGDON PRESS
NEW YORK   CINCINNATI   CHICAGO

Copyright, 1930, by
FLOYD W. LAMBERTSON

All rights reserved, including that of translation into foreign languages.
including the Scandinavian

Printed in the United States of America

AMERICA THE BEAUTIFUL[1]

O beautiful for spacious skies,
  For amber waves of grain,
For purple mountain majesties
  Above the fruited plain!
    America! America!
  God shed his grace on thee
And crown thy good with brotherhood
  From sea to shining sea!

O beautiful for pilgrim feet,
  Whose stern, impassioned stress
A thoroughfare for freedom beat
  Across the wilderness.
    America! America!
  God mend thine every flaw,
Confirm thy soul in self-control,
  Thy liberty in law!

O beautiful for heroes proved
  In liberating strife,
Who more than self their country loved,
  And mercy more than life.
    America! America!
  May God thy gold refine
Till all success be nobleness
  And every gain divine!

O beautiful for patriot dream
  That sees beyond the years
Thine alabaster cities gleam
  Undimmed by human tears!
    America! America!
  God shed his grace on thee
And crown thy good with brotherhood
  From sea to shining sea!

        —Katharine Lee Bates.

---

[1] Reprinted by permission of the author.

CONTENTS

	PAGE
"Purple Mountain Majesties Above the Fruited Plain"..................Frontispiece	
"America the Beautiful"...................	5
Foreword	9
The Man Who Was Prepared..............	11
The Ne'er-Do-Well......................	15
The Hero of the Cattle Range...........	21
A Girl Saves the Life of a General.......	26
The Unsung Hero......................	31
The Penalty of His Deeds................	37
An Irreverent Monarch Humbled.........	41
The Master Who Forgave................	45
The Heroine of the Shoshones...........	50
The Avenger of the Acadians.............	57
The Stranger's Gift.....................	62
The Beloved Disciple....................	68
The Gamin of Paris.....................	72
Sir Galahad............................	77
Paulus the Cobbler.....................	83
A King in Rags and a Beggar on the Throne..	87
A Champion of the Poor.................	92
The King Who Learned Kindness..........	97
Joan of Arc............................	101
The Song of the Shepherd King...........	107
Abe Lincoln's Happy Thanksgiving.........	112

CONTENTS

	PAGE
STRONG IN VICTORY AND BRAVE IN DEFEAT	116
A HEROIC FRIENDSHIP	120
THE MAID OF BETHLEHEM	126
THE MAN WHO BETRAYED HIS COUNTRY	131
THE HERO OF THE FEVER ZONE	134
KINDNESS REWARDED	139
FRIEND OF THE FRIENDLESS	144
THE BELOVED BISHOP	149
THOSE WHO LOVE THE FLAG	155

FOREWORD

THESE stories of courage, patriotism, loyalty, helpfulness, and reverence are intended to help in the character education of the Junior child. Many of them have a biblical background, though myth and fable have also been included.

They can be used advantageously in the problem-story method of teaching. The average child has a feeling of reverence for God, but his social adjustments are the danger zone in character making. Before or after a story is read let the children enter into a free and frank discussion of their own problems. Their life interests should be the focal point of all teaching.

As "Guess Who Stories" they may be used with good effect, the story being told without the name of the hero or heroine and the children being asked to find the name and be ready to retell the story at the next meeting.

Whether put into the hands of the children for individual reading, or used by leaders and teachers, the aim of the author will be fulfilled if the lives of boys and girls may be more and more motivated by the ideals set forth in the stories.

The author is indebted to Miss Katharine Lee

FOREWORD

Bates for permission to print her poem "America the Beautiful," and to the Educator Supply Co., of Mitchell, South Dakota, for permission to use two stories from their publications.

FLOYD W. LAMBERTSON.

THE MAN WHO WAS PREPARED

THE sand dunes silvered in the moonlight and the dark pines stood straight and tall along the shore of Lake Michigan, where a group of boys were spending their last night in camp. For the past two hours they had been having a spirited game of Prisoner's Goal; dark figures flitting through the shadows as the boys attempted to capture one of their enemies and carry him away to their well-guarded prison. Happy was the lad who brought in a prisoner.

But now the game was over and the boys had returned to their camp. A broad path of light gleamed across the water from their roaring camp fire. It was time for the story hour.

"Hurray for the cook," shouted James, looking hungrily toward the cook shack.

"Hurray for Tobin," shouted another, as their leader came into the group. Within a minute the woods were ringing with "Nine rahs, Tobin."

"I hope you have had a good time, boys."

"We have, we have," came from all sides.

"This is the last story hour we shall have before we break camp," said Tobin, "and I want to tell you about Moriarty, the man who was prepared. A few years ago the Tigers of Detroit were playing the team from Cleveland. It was an important game, as the team that won would

WORLD OVER STORIES

most surely go into the world championship series. Each man was playing his best.

"So evenly matched were they that at the beginning of the ninth inning the score was three to three. The Cleveland team came up for their last bat and were put out without scoring. Now came the turn of the Tigers. If they could rally and make one score the game was won.

"Moriarty was the first man to bat. He gripped his club and waited. A fast ball sped straight over the plate and he made a safe hit just over second base.

"The next man made a sacrifice hit that put him on second. Another man fanned but he was able to get on to third.

"What should he do next? It was a fine thing to get to third, but he did not want to die there. Getting third never marked scores on the score board. If he was going to win that game, he must go on home.

"The next man to bat was Mullen. He was a poor hitter whose average was about .250, which meant that he hit a safe one about once in four times at bat. Moriarty could not expect much help from him. There was only one thing to do and that was to steal home—if that were possible.

"Moriarty began studying the pitcher. He was left-handed. He had a peculiar wind up that took about a second longer than the average pitcher in getting the ball into play. Then since he was left-handed he faced first base rather than

THE MAN WHO WAS PREPARED

third. This was a further advantage to Moriarty.

"One strike on Mullen. One ball. Two strikes.

"If anything was to be done it must be done at once. The catcher seemed to signal for a high ball. It would take a second to come down and tag a man on the plate. Moriarty watched the pitcher begin his wind up. He led off as far as he dared. When he was sure the pitcher was about to throw the ball he shot forward with the speed of the wind.

"A streak of white passed the plate. A man, one hundred and seventy pounds in weight, made that ninety-foot dash and slid for the plate.

"When the dust cleared, the umpire, with palms downward, told the thousands of rooters that Moriarty was safe. His run had won the game."

A loud cheer broke from the boys as Tobin finished. "Hurrah for Moriarty; nine rahs, Tigers," they shouted.

"I liked that story," continued Tobin, "but it is not finished yet. Perhaps the most important part is still to be told. I am wondering just *when* Moriarty won that sprint. Was it on that particular day when he dashed from third to home? Well, partly. But it was won probably more in the days long before that. A man in a crisis has to trust to the strength he has gained in earlier days.

"Moriarty knew such a test would come some time. He had trained carefully for it. Even as

WORLD OVER STORIES

a boy like you he had been getting ready. He had eaten wholesome food. He had slept in the fresh air and had drunk plenty of water. He had trained his muscles day after day to carry him with lightning speed from one base to the next. Because he was prepared he met this supreme test and won.

"Boys," continued Tobin, "you are now getting ready for such tests as that. You have been here swimming, running, passing your tests, and making your bodies physically strong. That is part of the preparation.

"Soon school will begin and you will be back at your books. I hope you will go at it with a will and be mentally alert to learn all you can. That is also a part of the preparation.

"But no lad is fully prepared for life who does not keep himself morally clean and straight. The boy who thinks impure thoughts is breaking training. The athlete who breaks training always has to pay. You can't afford to do that.

"A strong body, an alert mind, and moral purity—these are the best preparation for life. I want you to be numbered among the men who are prepared."

THE NE'ER-DO-WELL

ON the eve of the French Revolution four men sat beside the fireplace of Doctor Manette in London talking over the troubles that were brewing in France. On one side of the doctor sat his friend, Mr. Lorry, the banker. Darney, his son-in-law, sat on his left. Lounging in the background, as was his custom, was the ne'er-do-well, Sydney Carton.

"The rabble have taken the city of Paris," said Mr. Lorry, "and I fear grave trouble in the future."

"I expected it," replied the gray-haired doctor, who had been a political prisoner in the Bastille of Paris for eighteen years. "The wretched people have been abused and starved by the nobles for years and now they will take their revenge."

"Who can blame them?" asked Darney. "I have seen the poor people out in their fields all night long to drive away the game that would eat the crops. Why did they not shoot these animals? Because it was against the law of the nobles who wanted to hunt. Then I have seen whole groups of nobles ride over the fields of the poor in their hunting trips, utterly ruining the crops. Little wonder that the peasants are up in revolt."

"Yes, that is part of their miseries," answered Lorry. "A more grievous burden was the tax on salt. A person must have salt to maintain life. It was so expensive that the poor could scarcely buy it."

"Poor, enslaved people," mused Doctor Manette with a far-away look as he remembered his long years of torture in prison.

The group sat till midnight discussing the situation, little realizing that within a week they would all be thrust into the very heart of the carnage. The next day Mr. Lorry thought it advisable for him to go to Paris in order to protect his banking interests there. He left on the night boat.

Then came a letter to Darney from a trusted servant of his in France. Darney owned an estate there and this man had been thrown into prison for trying to collect the rents. His letter was a piteous appeal to Darney to save him.

"I must do what I can for him," said the man to himself. "It is probably a dangerous thing for me to venture into France, but I can't stay here and have him suffer." He sat down and dashed off a letter to his wife telling her of the conditions, then set out for Paris.

No sooner had Darney set foot on French soil than he was arrested by red-capped soldiers as an enemy of the New Republic. They took him to Paris and flung him into the dungeon of the prison, La Forge.

Doctor Manette and his daughter were dazed

THE NE'ER-DO-WELL

when they read the letter from Darney. They alone realized the danger that he was in. It seemed to them that the best way to help would be to go immediately to Paris. Accompanied by Carton they also left the next day.

As they entered the city they got their first glimpse of the ruin brought about by the Revolutionists. These poor people, many of them thieves and robbers, were now masters of the city. Nothing was safe from their hatred. Guilty and innocent alike were beheaded. The days were made hideous by their war cries and the nights were scenes of terror. They stormed the royal palace and led the king and his family to the guillotine. Night skies were constantly lighted by the burning homes of the rich, and in this light men and women, clad in rags, danced through the streets, singing their wild songs in fiendish glee.

It was to such a place that Doctor Manette and his daughter came. The doctor himself was safe from their wrath, for he had been eighteen years a prisoner in the Bastille. In fact, he soon became the idol of the people. But when he asked for the freedom of Darney they turned a deaf ear. Darney was of noble blood; he had property and had oppressed the poor; let him suffer. The doctor could get no certain word as to his safety.

After weeks of weary waiting the day of Darney's trial came. He was ushered into the courtroom called the Hall of Blood. Here sat the judges on the bench, wearing their feathered hats. Here came the multitude, the rabble, awaiting new victims. Here also came Doctor Manette to plead the cause of his son-in-law.

With all eloquence he spoke of his own imprisonment, of the love he had for the poor, of his love for his daughter and her husband.

The people listened with interest as he told of his life in the Bastille. But when he spoke the name "Darney," they answered with sneers and hisses.

"Take off his head," they cried. "He is an enemy of the Republic."

In vain did the doctor plead with them for mercy. A verdict of "guilty" was quickly given and Darney was sentenced to die the next morning.

Sidney Carton sat in the judgment hall during the trial of his friend. He heard the cries of the people and the sentence of death. He left the room in deep thought.

"Why," he asked, "should Darney die? He has a wife and family who need him. I, Carton, am a ne'er-do-well, an idler, whose life has been a failure."

Suddenly there came to him a voice from the past. It was a verse he had learned from his mother's Bible, "Greater love hath no man than this, that a man lay down his life for his friends."

A beautiful smile overspread the face of Carton. He hastened away to Mr. Lorry and made him promise to have horse and carriage

THE NE'ER-DO-WELL

ready to quit France that very night. Lorry was to await his coming and to set out without asking a single question as soon as he should arrive. Lest he should lose his passport in the confusion of departure he gave it to Mr. Lorry for safe keeping.

Now Carton hurried away to a drug shop. He bought some chemicals. In the privacy of his own room he mixed and tested them. Then he sat down to await the approach of midnight.

At last the clock in the steeple tower tolled the hour of eleven. Carton dressed himself in high-topped boots and a long robe. Then he went in search of a cab.

"Drive me quickly to the prison, La Forge," he commanded. "Await my return and take me straight to the home of Doctor Manette. Here is your pay. Ask no questions."

Carton now mounted the stone steps of the prison. He whispered to one of the guards on duty and then was lost in the darkness. Together he and the guard climbed the winding stairs to the gloomy cell of Darney.

The condemned man was more than surprised to see his old friend, Carton. The two men clasped hands in a pledge of eternal friendship. They sat down on the stone bench under the flickering light of the guard's torch and talked over days gone by.

Darney never knew when he lost consciousness. He never knew when a pair of high boots were thrust onto his feet or a long black robe replaced his own coat. Neither did he know of a guard carrying him down the winding stairway to a waiting carriage. In fact, he was only partially himself when hours later he and his family and Mr. Lorry presented their passports at the border and crossed over to safety.

Back in the city of Paris, red-capped soldiers entered a gloomy cell the following morning, dragged forth a ne'er-do-well, and carted him away to the guillotine. Gallantly he gave up his life.

"Greater love hath no man than this, that a man lay down his life for his friends."

(Adapted from Dickens' *Tale of Two Cities*.)

THE HERO OF THE CATTLE RANGE

ON the plains of North Dakota, where the muddy Missouri winds its way through the Bad Lands, stood the ranch house of Theodore Roosevelt. It was a cold day in early spring. The sleet beat a steady tat-a-tat against the buildings and whipped through the cottonwoods. The gale without had little effect on the warmth and cheer of those within, however. Beside the large fireplace sat Roosevelt with his two companions, Sewell and Dowe, planning the spring work and talking over the local gossip.

"The vigilants are looking for the bad man Finnigan," drawled Sewell, stretching his legs comfortably toward the fire. "They say he is rustling [stealing] cattle up-country. They will string him to the nearest tree if they lay hands on him again." Such was the usual punishment for cattle thieves.

Roosevelt listened to the talk of the men. He said nothing and might have forgotten the matter entirely if Finnigan himself had not forced him to remember. The ranchmen had planned a trip across the river and had their packs and guns all ready for an early start the next morning. But when they went to the river the following day their boat was missing.

WORLD OVER STORIES

The three men stood on the bank in the raw March wind and looked over the situation.

"Finnigan," growled Sewell, eying the ground near the stake where the boat had been tied. "They say he has been moving southward. Rather handy," he added with growing anger, "to have a boat waiting for you like that."

"We must get that man," said Roosevelt in his determined way. "To let him go free will only encourage him and others to do lawless deeds. Lawbreakers must learn that punishment is swift and sure."

The men returned to the ranch house to plan their course of action. They must now build a raft. The thieves would hardly expect pursuit and would travel leisurely. They would soon be able to overtake them.

Two days later Roosevelt, Sewell, and Dowe stocked their unwieldy craft, carried their guns on board, and pushed off. The weather was intensely cold. Snow lay heavy on the ground and the wind bit to the bone. The ice jam had gone through the week previously and had left huge blocks of ice stranded along the shore. It was difficult to steer the raft. Their hands grew numb and their backs ached as they labored their way down the river through the red and purple butte land.

At the end of the third day they spied a small column of smoke circling from a thicket. They knew that they were nearing the end of their chase. They must move cautiously.

THE HERO OF THE CATTLE RANGE

"Hands up," said Roosevelt, suddenly stepping within the circle of the camp. The rustlers were taken completely by surprise. They made no resistance and within a few minutes were disarmed and tied.

"Let's give them the customary treatment and get on home," grumbled Sewell, looking at the sullen captives. Indeed, that was what they expected.

"No, we will let the law take its course," said Roosevelt. "There are laws in this State, and it is just as necessary that we obey the laws as that they do. They must be taken to jail and be tried in orderly fashion."

Sewell and Dowe looked at their employer in surprise.

They foresaw real difficulty ahead. To get three prisoners, who were now desperate, to some far-away prison, whose location was, as yet, unknown, was not going to be the easiest task in the world.

"The law for handling rustlers is pretty well fixed," said Dowe.

"Yes, but we would be lawbreakers in doing it that way. We must have them tried in regular fashion," answered Roosevelt.

The men made no further comment but settled down as comfortably as possible for the night.

On the following day they struck southward in the boat. Their plan was to float down the river to some town, turn the men over to the officers of the law, and return home. But within a day they came up with the ice jam and all progress was blocked. Now they must sit and wait for the jam to break.

New difficulties arose. Their food began to run low. All the men were put on half rations. Each day either Roosevelt or Sewell or Dowe set out in search of game, but the desolate plains rewarded them nothing. At last they were reduced to flour and water.

"I guess we ought to treat the prisoners in the customary way," smiled Dowe as he crouched near the fire that evening. "We will be entirely out of food in a short time."

"Not until all the food is gone," came Roosevelt's quick response. "We must try to find a ranch somewhere near. Perhaps we can get food and a team."

The next day Dowe scouted the country toward the east in search of a ranch. He came back in the evening unsuccessful. The men ate their unleavened bread in silence and crept in between their blankets for another uncomfortable night.

The following day Roosevelt started westward in search of a ranch. Late in the afternoon he sighted one and was soon supplied with a team and wagon and food. The next morning the prisoners were bumping across the frozen plains in a buckboard toward the county jail in Dickinson, some seventy miles away.

It had taken two weeks of strenuous effort and three hundred miles of travel to bring these

THE HERO OF THE CATTLE RANGE

prisoners to jail. But the hero of the cattle range set an example to the men of his community that the law must take its course and that the law must be obeyed.

A GIRL SAVES THE LIFE OF A GENERAL

SHE was a little Jewess named Rebecca. Her home was in the land of Israel on the fertile Plain of Esdraelon. There in her vine-clad cottage she helped her mother with the household duties or labored with her father in the fields.

Now trouble came to this happy family. The Syrian king raised an army and marched into the lake regions of Israel. Cruel soldiers burned her home and carried her away to Syria as a captive.

By good fortune she was taken to the home of the Syrian general, Naaman. She became waiting maid of the great general's wife. Although she often longed for her home and the quiet fields of Israel she learned to love her mistress, the wife of Naaman.

One day she came upon her in tears.

"You are sad, my mistress," she said. "Is there anything I can do to help you?"

"No, my child, there is nothing," she answered. "Naaman, my husband, has the dreadful disease, leprosy. It grows steadily worse. Some day he will be taken from me," sobbed the woman.

"Have faith, for he can be healed," said Rebecca.

A GIRL SAVES A GENERAL

"What is that you say?" cried her mistress, thinking she had misunderstood.

"Only have faith and he shall be healed," said Rebecca, more boldly. "Let him go to my country and to the prophet, Elisha, and he may be cured of his leprosy."

Naaman's wife went quickly to him with the words of Rebecca.

"It is useless," he said sadly, listening to the strange words of his wife. "Leprosy is a disease that cannot be cured."

"But, my husband, there can be no harm in trying," pleaded his wife.

Naaman told the words of the Jewish maid to the king of Syria.

"Indeed we will try," he said at once, hearing Naaman's message. "My brave general shall not die of leprosy if there is anything I can do."

Within a week Naaman was fitted out with a caravan for the journey to Israel. He bore a letter to the king, together with six thousand pieces of silver, ten pieces of gold, and ten changes of royal garments. In due time he arrived before the palace and a little later stood in the presence of the Israelitish king.

"What is this that the Syrian king asks of me?" cried the king of Israel, rending his clothes, "Thinks he that I am able to kill and make alive, to bring disease and cure it? He is but seeking a quarrel against me," and the king told Naaman that his quest was useless.

But Elisha, prophet of God, had learned of

the Syrian general's request and how the king of Israel had turned him away.

"Wherefore hast thou rent thy clothes, and why art thou troubled?" Elisha asked of the king. "Only send him to me and he shall know that there is a God in Israel."

This message was carried to Naaman as he was planning to return home. As a last resort he turned his caravan toward the humble home of the prophet.

Now, Naaman was a proud man. He had long dealt with nobles and kings and felt that his dealings with others should be done in proper form. He expected that his cure, if it should be made, would be accomplished with great display. Imagine his surprise when Elisha sent a servant to give the remedy. And that remedy was to wash seven times in the Jordan.

"Have I made this journey only to be laughed at?" cried the general in anger. "Behold, I supposed that this prophet would come out and call upon the name of his god, and go through certain rites. Now he tells me to bathe in the dirty River Jordan. To horse and let us be gone!"

Then one of his servants came to Naaman and said, "O Master, let us at least try what he has suggested. If he had asked a great thing, would you not have done it? But he says only, 'Wash and be clean.'"

"Very well, we will try," said Naaman reluctantly.

A GIRL SAVES A GENERAL

Now they went to the River Jordan. Naaman alighted and dipped in the warm waters. Once, twice, three times. He looked at his flesh and it was just as it had been before. Four times. Five times. Six times.

"Are not the rivers in my own country better than this dirty stream?" he cried, seeing his flesh unchanged.

"Only try once more," said his trusted servant.

So Naaman dipped the seventh time, when behold, his flesh became soft and smooth as the flesh of a little child.

"Cured!" cried the general exultantly, "cured of my leprosy! Behold, now I know that there is no god in all the earth save the God of Israel."

Quickly he returned to the home of the prophet.

"Come forth, O prophet, that I may repay you for your kindness! Here are six thousand pieces of silver and ten pieces of gold that are yours for the asking."

But Elisha would take no pay for this miraculous deed.

Then Naaman set out for home. Within a few days he reached his palatial residence and stood before his wife. All were overjoyed at his restoration to health.

"Bring forth the little Jewess. Bring forth Rebecca," commanded the general. "To her belongs the credit for telling me of this wonderful prophet."

When Rebecca stood before him he said: "My

child, I owe you much for your kindness. You are free. Return to the land of your fathers if you desire."

"The Lord lift up his countenance upon thee and give thee peace," she replied.

THE UNSUNG HERO

IN the days of the long-forgotten past there lived in northern Europe a mighty race of warriors called the Volsungs. These brave warriors spent their winters among the snow-clad forests of the north. There by their fjords they feasted in their huge log houses or hunted the game in the woodland. But with the coming of spring they would mend their boats and proudly sail away to conquer some distant country.

Chiefest among this lordly race was their king, Sigmund, beloved of friends and feared of foes. He with his gentle wife, Seiglunde, held sway over these sea-faring warriors. But most beloved of the parents and the idol of the people was the little son, Siegfried.

"Take good care of my son," would be the father's parting command as he strode toward the deck of his vessel. "Train him in the ways of valor and honor. Some day he must be king in my stead."

The welfare of the young prince became the chief concern of the mother. From the days of his babyhood she lavished all her love upon him. All his clothes were made by her loving hands. She prepared for him the most nourishing foods. She tucked him to sleep at night with a story of some great hero among his ancestors.

Then as he grew older others helped in training him. He was taught to hurl the javelin and to wield the battle-ax. He learned to hunt in the dark forest, and knew the ways of the animals. Wise men came from far to give him of their wisdom, for he was to become a mighty monarch and must be properly prepared.

Siegfried responded well to his training. He could outrun his young companions, and showed greater accuracy in shooting with the bow and arrow. He became a famous hunter even in his youth, and many a narrow escape did he have as with his father he followed the stag through the heart of the forest.

"Do you see that smoke ascending?" asked the father one day as they returned from the chase. "That is the home of our master craftsman, Mimir the Mighty. He is the most skilled smith in the world. It is he who forges the swords with which we defeat our enemies. Some day you too must go to labor at the forge. A true nobleman believes in honest toil."

So it came about that later Siegfried left his comfortable home and went to live on the hard fare of Mimir. Amidst the din of ringing anvils, the smoke and flying sparks, he took his place as an apprentice and did the humble tasks of a beginner. Now he wore the coarse leathern apron and wooden shoes of a peasant. His food was largely soup and black bread. But he enjoyed the labor and quickly became a skilled workman.

On a certain day Mimir came to the shop with

THE UNSUNG HERO

a look of grave concern. He called his helpers about him and told them his plight. In a neighboring kingdom lived another smith, Amilias the Burgundian. This man had challenged him to mortal combat. He had made a coat-of-mail of such excellent steel that no sword could pierce it. Now he challenged Mimir to make a sword that would strike through it. If Mimir could not do so, he was to become an underling at the forge of Amilias. Mimir had tried for many days to fashion such a sword but his efforts had been useless. He appealed to his apprentices to help him.

One after another began to make excuses. Surely, if the master could not make such a sword they would be unable to do it. When all the others had spoken, Siegfried, the youngest, said, "Master, I can make a sword that will defeat this proud Burgundian. May I try?"

Permission was gladly given. Siegfried left the group and went in search of the best steel that could be had. Now for three days he labored at his forge amid the smoke and flying sparks until he had a sword after his liking. This he took to the master.

But even as they tested the sword Siegfried was dissatisfied with it and broke it over his knee. He returned to the forge to begin his labors anew.

A week passed. A second time the youth brought a sword to his master. This was of much finer quality and they gave it a thorough test. Going to a nearby brook Mimir threw onto the water a handful of wool. Then as the current bore it down stream he held the sword at the water's edge. The blade of the sword was so keen that it parted the wool as though it had been a single thread.

"Well done, my son," said the swarthy blacksmith as he bent the blade back to the hilt. "Well done, indeed. This blade is sharp enough to cleave the steel of Amilias."

But Siegfried was yet dissatisfied.

"Let me but try again," he said, and returned to his forge.

Now for seven weeks there came the steady ring of the hammer on the anvil and the bright glow of the fire. No one was permitted to go near the forge of Siegfried and none knew the magic that was wrought into the blade. On one occasion the other apprentices thought they saw a strange man come to the forge in the dusk of the twilight and pass to Siegfried glittering pieces of metal. But as they came toward him he vanished from sight. And ever the clang of the anvil continued.

At length, haggard and weary, Siegfried came forth bearing a sword wondrously wrought. On the handle were runic rimes and mystic symbols that bespoke the mighty days of old. Placing it in the hands of Mimir, he cried:

"Behold, the sword, Balmung. Behold the glittering terror. That shall conquer our foes."

Seizing it by the hilt the youth twirled it in air and then struck the anvil on which he had

THE UNSUNG HERO

worked. It fell to the ground in two pieces but the blade of the sword was uninjured.

"It will do," said the master, quietly.

On the following day an answer was sent to Amilias the Burgundian. Messengers sped to all parts of the Lowlands saying that on a certain day, Mimir, master smith of the Volsungs, would meet Amilias of the Burgundians to decide who was the greatest smith in the world.

The day of the contest came. On the broad plain bordering the two countries thousands of people were assembled. The Burgundian king and his retinue took their place on the grassy slopes toward the eastward.

Toward the west were king Sigmund and his doughty Volsungs. Siegfried stood near his father's throne and watched the scene with beating heart.

Now amid a blare of trumpets Amilias strode out of his group, clad in his coat of mail, and took his position in the center of the plain. With proud boasts he challenged Mimir to come forth.

Then from the ranks of the Volsungs came the small figure of Mimir. A roar of laughter from the Burgundians greeted his advance.

As they came together in the middle of the plain there was a mighty silence.

"Are you ready?" asked Mimir as he reached his huge opponent.

"Strike," answered Amilias.

Mimir raised his sword and twirled it in air for a minute while the rays of the sun flashed like

WORLD OVER STORIES

lightning from its surface. Then he brought it down across the breast of the giant. The man was severed completely in two.

A great shout burst from the Volsungs. Their smith had proved his might. He had made the sword which overthrew their haughty foe. He was borne back toward the throne in triumph.

For a moment a feeling of bitter resentment flashed through the mind of Siegfried. Mimir was receiving the credit for the work he had done. All were speaking words of praise for the master craftsman, even the king and queen, but not a word was said of his seven weeks of toil.

"Surely Mimir will tell who made the sword," thought Siegfried, as he crowded near the throne. But not a word did Mimir say, and the apprentices did not speak.

The young prince felt a throb of pain as he realized that another was to receive all the credit for the work he had done.

But as he moved away he had a feeling of true joy and happiness. He had made that sword. By his own toil and painstaking effort he had fashioned the sword that brought victory to his nation. What cared he who got the credit? Success was not to be measured by the applause of the people. It was to be found in the knowledge that he had done his best. That thought was his greatest reward. And with that thought he was supremely happy.

(From the Norse mythology.)

THE PENALTY OF HIS DEEDS

INCHCAPE ROCK. A hidden reef. The boom of the surf. A storm and shipwreck in the night. Sailors clinging to bits of driftwood. This is but an imperfect picture of a scene that occurred only too frequently at a spot on the northern coast of Scotland. Here, only a short distance from the bold bluff, lay concealed a reef known as Inchcape Rock. This jagged bowlder was in the regular channel just below the surface and many an unwary sailor steered his ship upon it. The fisherfolk soon came to have a superstitious dread of the place. To them it seemed that an evil genius dwelt there waiting to grasp the poor sailor.

So great was the loss of life that finally the monks built an abbey on the bluff. They hoped that by being near the spot in the time of storm they might rescue some of the sailors. Through their efforts scores of lives were saved.

Then there came to the abbey a new Abbot who conceived a better plan.

"Brothers," he said, "you have done good work in helping the shipwrecked seamen. But you are only trying to remedy the damage after it has been done. Let us now build a buoy on Inchcape Rock and place a bell inside it. When the waves roll the bell will ring and warn the sailors from the dangerous spot."

WORLD OVER STORIES

The words of the Abbot were gladly received by the monks. They saw at once that their task would not be an easy one. First, they must build a raft on which to work. Then they must bore a hole deep into the heart of the rock so that they could fasten the buoy securely.

The work was begun. Day after day relays of monks toiled away on the raft, sinking the hole deeper and deeper. At length they felt that they could sink their cable and fasten the buoy to its top. With this done they returned to their abbey to await results.

Within a week a terrific storm arose. Now through the noise and din of the waves could be heard the deep-toned knelling of the bell warning the ships from the hidden reef. And in the following years many a mariner breathed a blessing on the Abbot and his monks for placing this buoy on Inchcape Rock.

Then it chanced that Roger the Rover sailed through these waters. He was a bold, bad man whose chief delight was in bringing sorrow and misery to others. He with his pirate crew roamed the seven seas, robbing the passing merchantmen. Happening to sail along the northern Scottish coast he spied the Inchcape bell. An evil smile crept over his face.

"Men," shouted Sir Roger in his hoarse voice, "down with the small boat and row me over to the Inchcape Rock. Methinks it will ring for the fishes from now on."

The boat was launched and made its way

THE PENALTY OF HIS DEEDS

toward the rock. As it touched the wooden frame which the hands of the monks had fashioned the Rover leaned over and cut the cable which held it to its place. With gurgling sound the bell sank beneath the waves and was seen no more. The Rover gave a reckless laugh and sailed away in search of new adventure.

Weeks and months passed by. The Rover sailed his ship toward the rich gold mines of Mexico. He plied his trade so successfully that soon his ship was full to overflowing with the nuggets of gold. It seemed to him and his men that they had sufficient wealth to live happily for the rest of their lives. Therefore they turned their ship homeward.

The heart of the Rover was glad. The weather was fine and the doughty little vessel skimmed along the rolling waves with rapid pace. But as they neared the English coast the weather turned treacherous. Skies were overcast and fogbanks piled up along the horizon. Roger knew that a storm was brewing. At length it broke in all its fury and the pirate ship was compelled to run with the wind.

"Where are we?" demanded Sir Roger of his helmsman one dark night.

"I know not for sure," said the helmsman, fearfully. "'Methinks we cannot be far from the Scottish coast and probably near the Inchcape Rock."

"Breakers ahead," came the cry of the watchman on deck.

WORLD OVER STORIES

All listened with breathless attention. Straight ahead of them came the unmistakable sound of the breakers. Then a flash of lightning rent the heavens and gave a glimpse of the distant shore.

"The Abbey of Abertbrothok!" shouted the helmsman. "We are headed for the hidden reef!"

Sir Roger trod the deck in anger and fear. His ship was laden with much treasure and now it seemed that he might lose out in this fight with the elements. The wind shrieked through the rigging as it drove them on toward the shore.

"There is still hope if we can avoid the Inchcape Rock," shouted the helmsman. "If only we knew exactly where it lay!"

The Rover thought of the day when with reckless laugh he had cut the bell from its moorings. Now he wished it was there to warn them of the hidden rock.

Suddenly there came a mighty crash. The ship shuddered in every beam and groaned as though in torment. There came the sound of water rushing through the rent in her side. She reeled a moment, then began to sink.

"O God," shrieked Roger, tearing his hair, "that I should lose my fortune here on this accursed rock! Truly my evil deed is returning upon my own head."

With a plunge the ship sank below the waves.

(Adapted from Southey's poem,
"The Inchcape Rock.")

AN IRREVERENT MONARCH HUMBLED

IN the sunny land of Sicily once lived a proud monarch, King Robert. It was his custom, when the bells in the vaulted tower tolled the hour of worship, to go to the cathedral and take his place among the people. He came to this service, however, with no thought of worship. This haughty man loved neither God nor his fellows. He looked with contempt upon the unfortunate and despised the poor of his realm. His only concern was that his money chambers be full and that he should not be disturbed by the affairs of state.

A smile played over his face as he saw others kneel in prayer. Then he heard the words of the leader—"He humbleth the mighty in their conceit and the poor he exalteth."

"What are these words they are saying?" cried the king with a sneer. "Who can humble me, Robert of Sicily? I fear no harm from either God, man, or devils." So saying he settled back into his seat and fell asleep.

It was black night when he awoke. The darkened cathedral echoed with strange and weird sounds as he groped his way toward the entry. No courtiers were there to assist him. The angry monarch flung off his outer robes and

WORLD OVER STORIES

rushed along the street. Coming to his palace he thrust aside the attendants and plunged on toward the royal chambers, where a banquet was about to be served.

Robert paused a moment at the threshold looking about him at the scene of splendor. Nobles and ladies were already assembled. The tables were loaded with delicate foods.

Then the king looked toward the throne on the raised dais. There, in his place, sat another, his exact likeness in form and figure. It was in truth an Angel in disguise, though the king knew it not.

"Down with that false man," shouted the enraged Robert, stalking forward into the room. "I am Robert, King of Sicily, and this one would usurp my throne."

Men-at-arms and attendants seized him and held him back.

"A madman has escaped from prison," said the Angel. "But since he thinks himself of royal blood, let us crown him as King of the Jesters. Bring forth cap and bells and let him make merry for us."

A shout of laughter came from the assembled guests at this suggestion.

"For his companion he shall have the hairy ape of the courtyard," continued the Angel, "and his labor shall be that of serving the menials of the palace and stables."

The proud monarch was quickly arrayed in cap and bells. His wrist was chained to that

A MONARCH HUMBLED

of a huge ape. He must follow this beast wherever it went.

Such strange companions caused much amused interest among the servants as well as among the nobles. Pages and kitchen-maids shouted in merriment. Townspeople followed the pair with crude jest and cruel joke. When Robert flung back his wrathful answers, they but teased him the more.

The disgrace of such a life seared the soul of the once haughty monarch as with fire. In fury he answered his tormentors. When the Angel met him some months later and spoke of his former position he shouted, "Impostor, I am, I *am* the king."

One year rolled by, then a second. Robert was forced to help the most humble servants of kitchen and stable. He learned for the first time of the sufferings and sorrows of the poor. He began to have a heartfelt sympathy for these unfortunates.

Now Robert thought seriously of his days as a king. He began asking himself why he had been proud and haughty. Wherein was he superior to those about him? Other men needed food and clothes just as he did. Others felt joy and sorrow just as he did. All men, everywhere, longed for the sympathy and good will of their fellows. Every man was dependent on God for his daily bread.

As the king saw how shallow and false his pride had been he thrust it from him as being

WORLD OVER STORIES

unworthy of a true monarch. Now he found a real satisfaction in helping others. Many a troubled servant came to him for advice and found new hope and courage in his wise counsels.

And now, when the bells rang in the cathedral tower, this man, in true reverence, stood with bowed head in the courtyard.

"Are you still the king?" asked the Angel one day as they passed on the stairway.

"I am the most sinful and needy of men," he answered humbly.

"My task is done," said the Angel. "'Tis time you were restored to your throne. Come and I will robe you in your royal purple again."

So saying he led the way to the royal chambers. Now Robert put off his coarse clothes and was dressed again in his regal splendor.

From that day forth Robert of Sicily became a true ruler of his people. His kindly spirit won their hearts. No monarch in all the surrounding kingdoms was held in higher regard. He had learned that love for God and kindly service are the true marks of a noble character.

> (Based on Longfellow's poem,
>   "Tales of a Wayside Inn.")

THE MASTER WHO FORGAVE

"COME up here. Step lively, you young giant," shouted the slave auctioneer, cracking his whip.

A huge Phrygian slave slowly mounted the auction block.

"How much am I bid? What will you give? Step right up, gentlemen, and look him over."

It was in the market place of the once thriving city of Colosse that this scene occurred.

"What? Let this fine offer go? Here is a bargain, a real bargain. How much am I bid?"

The slave looked with weary eyes over the assembled throng. Suddenly his eyes glowed like smoldering coals as he caught a glimpse of the rugged Cadmus mountains that backed up the city. If he could only break these shackles on his feet and once gain their craggy peaks.

"He is young, he is powerful. He will make you a valuable slave," again rang out the harsh voice of the auctioneer.

About this time two new members joined the crowd. They were Philemon, wealthy landowner of Colosse, and his son, Archippus. They listened as one bid after another was made.

"Father, let's buy this slave," said Archippus. "Some way, I feel sorry for him; he seems so big and helpless. Possibly too he can be taught to love the Christ."

WORLD OVER STORIES

Just at this instant an incident occurred which turned the tables. In a moment of pause, the auctioneer, with the skill that is common to his trade, turned to the slave.

"What is your name?" he asked.

"My name is Onesimus," was the reply.

It so happens that "Onesimus" is a Greek word which means "useful," or "profitable." The auctioneer took advantage of this name as a selling point.

"Buy this slave; buy this slave," he shouted, again cracking his whip. "His name tells you the kind of man he is. It is Onesimus, the useful, the profitable. Who raises the bid?"

The upshot of it was that Philemon bought the young Phrygian and took him home.

Onesimus quickly fitted into the life of the plantation. Whether in the city home of his master or working in the fertile fields that fronted the Lycus River his strength plus his good common sense made him a most valuable helper. As the days passed by his master began giving him special privileges and greater freedom than the other slaves enjoyed. He showed himself perfectly trustworthy. Especially was Archippus pleased because of his interest in the services held each Sunday.

It so happened that Philemon and his family had become Christians due to the preaching of the great apostle Paul. After that worthy man had left their community, Archippus himself was appointed as pastor and spoke each Sunday to

THE MASTER WHO FORGAVE

those who gathered in his own home. Onesimus was always an interested listener on these occasions.

But one morning the plantation overseer came up to Philemon to say that their "profitable" slave had stolen a goodly sum of money during the night and was gone. No trace could be found of him.

In the meantime Onesimus boarded a sailing vessel bound for Rome. He felt sure that he could lose himself in that great city. As soon as he set foot in Rome he made his way to the Suburba, where the poorer people lived. So long as his money lasted he had a gay time. Aside from his own brawls there were the games in the arena.

But now his money gave out. Onesimus wandered the streets penniless and alone. His conscience began to bother him. He thought of the kind master he had left and of the privileges he had given over.

One day as he was aimlessly roaming around he saw a group of people entering a private dwelling. He followed them in. There, before him, sat a small man in chains with a Roman soldier standing on each side. This man was talking—talking of one Jesus, the Christ.

"Jesus; Jesus the Christ," said Onesimus. "Ah, that is the name that Archippus spoke so often."

The lonely slave sat quietly during the talk of this man. He found out that this was Paul, the

WORLD OVER STORIES

great apostle, who was now a prisoner of the emperor. At the close of the service Paul spoke to him.

"What is your name, my friend?" asked the aged apostle.

"I am Onesimus, and I heard of you in the house of my master, Philemon, in Colosse," he replied.

"Philemon and Archippus?" exclaimed the teacher. "Why, they are my friends. It was I who first told them of the blessed Christ and made Archippus the teacher of Colosse."

The friendless runaway slave now broke down and told Paul his past history. He was sorry for having taken money from his kind master but feared to return because of the severe punishment often meted out to runaway slaves.

"Never fear, my friend," said Paul. "I will see that no harm befalls you. I will write to Philemon myself and beg for your forgiveness. Remain here with me until you find a boat ready to sail for Colosse."

A stanch friendship now grew up between the slave and the prisoner. Paul would gladly have had him remain in Rome as his helper, but, as he adds in his letter to Philemon, "without thy mind I would do nothing." Later in the letter Paul referred to the theft. "If he hath wronged thee at all, or oweth thee aught, put that to mine account."

With such a letter Onesimus set sail from Rome for Colosse. It was with fear and trem-

THE MASTER WHO FORGAVE

bling that he made his way to the home of Philemon. But when the latter had read Paul's letter he received his slave gladly.

"I forgive you of your past deed," he said kindly, "and may your future life prove that you are truly 'profitable.'"

"Indeed it shall," said Onesimus, and he lived up to his word.

(Based upon the letter to Philemon in the New Testament.)

THE HEROINE OF THE SHOSHONES

FAR away in the mountains of Idaho there once lived a powerful chieftain of the Shoshone Indians by the name of Heawit. The wigwams of five hundred braves were sheltered in the mountain strongholds and were safe for the winter. This mighty warrior now spent his time in his own lodge, and after the work of the day loved best to sink back among the deep furs of his couch and listen to the love songs of his little daughter.

"Come, little bird; come, my bird song, sing for me," he would say of an evening.

Then the little child would come out before the burning embers in the center of the lodge and begin with her bell-like tone to sing him the songs he most loved. Frequently she would accompany her songs with rhythmic movement similar to the dances of the people at times of festivals.

As the smoke circled upward toward the deep shadows of the roof and the last note of her song had died away, the chief would rouse from his dream and say, "You are indeed my bird song, my bird woman. Your name shall be Sacajawea."

In this way did the little child come to have the name of Bird Woman, or Sacajawea.

THE HEROINE OF THE SHOSHONES

Little Sacajawea became the idol of the tribe. Not only did she sing for her father but for others, the aged and sick. She loved to go among the tepees doing deeds of kindness for the people who were unable to help themselves. Her kindly deeds gained her the love and affection of the entire tribe.

But as she grew to young womanhood there occurred a great misfortune. The Minnetarees, another tribe from the Knife River district, were the sworn enemies of the Snake Indians, the Shoshones. One spring these enemies went on the war path. Before Heawit was aware of their doings they had made a sudden raid into his fortress, burned many tepees, killed several of his braves, and carried away captive some of the women.

"Where is my bird song, where is my little Bird Woman?" moaned the father that night after the enemy had left. But he was not to see his child again.

However, her life was still to be one of helpfulness, although she could not know it. The Minnetarees sold her to the Mandans of North Dakota, and later she was married to a French trader, Charboneau.

Sacajawea never lost heart although she was far from home and among a strange tribe. Her song and good cheer and kindliness made friends for her wherever she went. Soon she was beloved by the members of her new home. After one year and then a second had passed she gave up

WORLD OVER STORIES

hope of ever returning to the tents of her people in the far-away mountains.

It was about this time that events in our country were happening which were to have a great effect upon her life. In 1803, President Jefferson decided to send out a party to the great Northwest Territory to find out the nature of the country and to set up trading posts if possible among the Indians. Lewis and Clark were chosen to lead the band. Some thirty men—hunters, trappers and guides—were to accompany them.

In 1804 they left Saint Louis and traveled northward up the Missouri River. Their boats skirted the lands of the treacherous Sioux Indians. Time after time they were halted in their advance by warlike bands, but in each case the courage and tact of their leaders got them through safely. By fall they had reached the Mandan tribes, and here they decided to camp for the winter.

Now new difficulties arose for the leaders. They were soon to strike westward through the less known country. They needed guides who knew the course of the rivers and who could speak the language of the tribes through whose territory they must pass.

"Who of your people can serve as guides?" asked Lewis and Clark of the Chief of the Mandans.

"My braves cannot help you," he replied, "for we have never gone so far west. Ask Char-

THE HEROINE OF THE SHOSHONES

boneau. He has been a trapper and hunter. He can help you."

So it came about that the leaders went to this French hunter, and asked if he would act as their guide. Sacajawea heard their request and decided that here was her best opportunity to return home to her people. Stepping before them she asked the leaders to include her among their number.

"I fear we cannot take you," said the leaders. "This will be a difficult trip and with your baby you will not be able to stand the hardship."

Sacajawea straightened up to her full height and answered them.

"Can you find food in the desert? Can you make the moccasins? Can you cure the sore eyes and keep the rattler's bite from causing death? Can you speak the language of the Shoshones? 'Tis there you want to go. I, Sacajawea, can lead you straight to the council fires of my people."

After due thought she was permitted to go with her husband. It was fortunate for the company that she was along. The helpful deeds of this Indian heroine must be writ large in the success of the venture.

In the spring of 1806 the company set sail again. Day after day they labored up the Missouri, sometimes having to row by hand, at others being favored by the wind. Before they had been gone a month they ran into the low, level plains of the Dakotas. Sometimes the land looked like lava from some burned-out volcano. Again the bluffs of yellow clay rose full a hundred feet from the banks. Game was scarce and they began to suffer want.

Now Sacajawea showed her knowledge. Going ashore she searched among the holes of the gophers. With a sharpened piece of driftwood she dug open their storehouses and gathered a large number of artichokes, similar in taste to the potato, which she brought to camp and prepared for food. Thus she saved the men from serious want.

Traveling further they approached the Great Falls of the Missouri in Montana. The water became more swift and the channel more narrow. Now the men must get out and drag the canoes with a rope. Many times they waded in the ice-cold water up to their arm-pits. When they could walk on shore, the rocks were so ragged and sharp that their moccasins were quickly worn out. It was Sacajawea whose willing hands fashioned new shoes from the hide of the buffalo.

Again on the warm days rattlesnakes lay basking in the sun on the rocks. Frequently the men were bitten. It was Sacajawea who knew a remedy for the snake bite.

On and on they went, forcing their canoes up the rapid current, dragging them overland around shallows and rapids, towing them by rope or poling them with long poles when the water was sufficiently shallow. Finally they came to a fork in the stream. Which branch should they

THE HEROINE OF THE SHOSHONES

take? If they chose the wrong one, they would waste many precious days.

Sacajawea advised the more southerly stream. That, she said, led toward the tents of her tribe. After exploring a bit, Lewis and Clark decided on the southern branch. Now they were coming nearer to her home. This for Sacajawea was a great joy, but for the leaders it was a time of doubt and dread. They knew that they must carry their goods from the headwaters of the Missouri to the Columbia River. The Shoshones controlled the country through which they must pass. What if they would refuse them passage?

"Come; my father or my brother is now chieftain. Let me but speak to him and you shall find passage." Thus this Indian woman encouraged them.

Great was her joy as they came to the "Gates of the Mountain." Huge, frowning cliffs of black granite rose twelve hundred feet sheer above the water's edge. Just beyond them were certain rocks that seemed white in appearance.

"'Tis here my people get the white for their war paint," she told them.

At last the great day came. Swiftly Sacajawea made her way through the mountain pass toward the home of her father. He was now dead and Cameahwait, her brother, was chief in his stead. She wept for sheer joy as she stood once more among her people.

"Come, pale-face friends," said this warrior to

WORLD OVER STORIES

the members of the company. "Come, we will aid you in any way possible."

A royal welcome was given to the members of the party. The horses they needed to carry their baggage to the headwaters of the Columbia were soon brought and they were again on their way.

We need not tell of the trip of Lewis and Clark down the Columbia nor of their stay on the Pacific Coast. When they returned, the following year, it was Sacajawea and her husband who guided them back over the trail toward the white man's country.

In due time, Lewis and Clark returned to Washington and gave their report to President Jefferson. They were loud in their praise of the Bird Woman, Sacajawea, whose words of cheer and helpful deeds had helped to make the great expedition possible.

THE AVENGER OF THE ACADIANS

THE little village of Grand Pré, on the west coast of Nova Scotia, still holds a charm and beauty for the traveler. How much more was this true in the long-ago days when the sturdy French Acadians tilled their broad acres and garnered their abundant harvests!

The early history of this little community began shortly after 1600, when a group of Acadians came to these shores. Sailing up the long Bay of Fundy, they passed the thundering Cape Blomidon and viewed the smooth tablelands before them.

"This shall be our home," said their leader. "Here we can live free from tyranny and oppression."

So it came about that the village of Grand Pré had its birth. Soon thatch-roofed cottages also dotted the valley and the fragrance of thousands of apple blossoms hung like incense in the balmy spring air.

It was many years later that Pierre, the blacksmith, built his forge in the village. Here, as he made the heavy wagons or fashioned a plowshare, the men of the village would come to discuss local problems.

"I hear that France is again at war with England," said the smith one evening as he finished his work. "I like not these English and will never swear allegiance to them even if they should capture our land."

"Nor we, nor we," answered his friends. "We want no king save the good king of France. Long live the king! Long live our glorious homeland!"

The fortunes of war were unfavorable to these humble Acadians. The English won in the struggle and the land of Acadia became an English province.

True to their word, these peasants refused to swear allegiance to the British flag. They made no active resistance, for they were a peace-loving people, but they showed a feeling of hostility which annoyed the English. The victors feared lest they rise in revolt and welcome a French army into the heart of their province. It seemed to the war lords that these people should be taken from their land and scattered in the other provinces of the New World. Finally a decree was issued to this effect.

"What is the meaning of these ships in our harbor?" asked Pierre one evening of his comrades. "They sail the British flag and have their guns pointed shoreward. I like not their warlike intentions. Why should they come here troubling us?"

The following day Colonel Winslow, leader of the expedition, came ashore with his troopers and ordered all the Acadian men to assemble in their church at the hour of noon. When at length they

THE AVENGER OF THE ACADIANS

were all present and he had securely barred the doors the colonel spoke.

"It is a painful duty that I am called upon to perform," he said gravely, "but it is the command of my king. For the safety of our empire he commands that your lands be forfeited to the Crown and that you be deported to the southern colonies. God grant that you may find new homes there and become loyal subjects of his Majesty."

All was silent for a moment as the meaning of his words was gathered by these simple peasants. Then the storm broke.

"Down with the tyrants!" they shouted, rising to a man. "Down with this foreign foe! We will not give up our homes."

Blood would surely have been shed had not the much-loved pastor, Sebastian, rushed quickly forward.

"My children, my children," he said, raising his arms heavenward in entreaty, "what is it that you do? Would you commit murder here in the house of God? Let us forgive. Let us be patient. Remember the words of the blessed Christ who could say of his enemies, 'Father, forgive them, for they know not what they do.'" By such earnest entreaties did their beloved pastor quiet the tumult and avoid bloodshed.

Now began a period of mourning in the village. Word quickly spread of the command of the king. The fathers and husbands were not permitted to leave the church. It was commanded

WORLD OVER STORIES

that the mothers and children be ready to embark within three days. They were permitted to take only a few of their belongings, for the boats were too few for so large a company.

On the appointed day the populace gathered on the shore. The doors of the church were opened and the men marched toward the boats between lines of soldiers. With sad hearts they looked back at their thatched cottages in the valley and then set sail, many of them never to return.

The men were divided so that no large number were in any boat. But no sooner had they of the largest vessel been shoved into the hold than they began to talk of revolt. The young men counseled that they make a sudden sally against the soldiers at night, take over the ship, and put back toward their homeland.

"My children, my children," again pleaded their pastor, "we must do as our Master commanded and return good for evil. Two wrongs never make a right. Let us show kindness even to those who wronged us grievously."

The boats had not been long at sea when a tremendous storm arose. The water became one seething mass of waves and the ship pitched and tossed for a full week on the mighty Atlantic.

One morning the ship's captain was directing the work of some sailors when an iron cable struck him on the wrist. Although it pained him greatly he paid little attention to it. The second day it was badly swollen. On the third day he

THE AVENGER OF THE ACADIANS

was carried to his room in a raging fever. Infection had set in and they feared for his life.

The gentle pastor now came forward and offered his services. He had been the doctor of the village and was not unfamiliar with such cases. However, he had a hard task confronting him. The captain was stark mad with the fever. Time and again he would spring from his cot and start for the deck. It frequently required the combined strength of three men to keep him in his berth. Night after night, and day after day, the patient Sebastian stayed by his bedside, giving such remedies as the ship afforded.

Some weeks later the captain, pale and drawn, was able again to come on deck. His boat had now reached the southern seas not far from the mouth of the Mississippi. One fine day they docked along the wharves of New Orleans.

With feeble step the captain came to the gangplank and watched the Acadians leave the ship. When he saw the pastor approaching he drew him aside and asked what price he owed for the good man's services.

"Nothing at all, sir," said the aged pastor, "nothing at all. The blessed Christ has commanded us to do deeds of kindness to anyone in need. He has taught us to return good for evil. By these deeds of mercy I am become the avenger of the Acadians."

(Based upon Longfellow's poem,
"Evangeline.")

THE STRANGER'S GIFT

ON the edge of a small village in the Black Forest of Germany there once lived an aged woodcutter and his family. Each day the father and son went into the dark forest, there to fell the trees and prepare them for market. Loading them into their crude cart, they hauled them to the distant city. In this way they made enough money to buy their food.

But this spring they had met difficulty. The horse that always pulled their cart became lame, and as they could not get their wood to market, they were without money or food.

"I hope we have a big supper to-night," said the clumsy Johann as they finished their day's work. "I want lots to eat."

"I'm afraid there will not be much," answered the father. "Only this morning mother said we had enough flour to last for supper and breakfast. When that is gone we must trust the good Lord for more." The old man sighed as he thought of the future.

The men gathered up their tools and started for home. As they entered the living room of their humble dwelling they found supper awaiting them.

"It is not much," said Gretchen, the mother, "but we must save enough for breakfast. Then the flour will be gone."

THE STRANGER'S GIFT

"Let's eat it all to-night," said the gluttonous Johann, "and let to-morrow take care of itself."

"That we must not do," said the father. "You will be as hungry to-morrow as you are now."

But if anyone had watched, he would have seen the father break his rye cake in two and place half of it beside the plate of the son.

After supper father and son went out of doors to finish the work about the barn.

"We must get in a goodly supply of wood," said the father. "A storm is brewing. Bring in that big log, Johann. We will try to keep warm even though we have not much to eat."

Soon the ruddy glow of the fire warmed every nook and cranny of their little home while without the wind roared and drops of rain began beating on the roof.

As they were about to go to bed there came a loud knocking at the door.

"What? A stranger out on such a bad night?" said the father. "We must give him a welcome, in God's name." Flinging open the door he saw before him a man of middle age clad in rags and shivering with the cold.

"May I stay here for the night, friends?" he asked. "I tried to find lodging in the village but none had room for one so poor as I."

"Come right in," cried the father. "No man was ever turned away from our door. We have but little, but we share it gladly with those who are in need."

"Yes, and now there will not be anything left

WORLD OVER STORIES

for me to eat to-morrow," grumbled Johann to himself as he eyed the stranger. With that he stumbled off to bed.

The stranger entered and sank down before the warm fire. In the meantime the mother began preparing for their guest. Since there were not enough beds for all, they gave up theirs and made ready to sleep on the floor. This meant putting down some straw and placing a blanket over it.

"I am sorry to bother you," spoke the stranger as he noted their preparations, "but the night grew so bad I feared to go on into the forest."

"It is no bother at all," replied the old man, kindly. "The Good Book speaks about entertaining angels unawares, and we should not want to miss that chance. You are welcome to such comforts as we have."

Now it was time to go to bed. The guest had the room of the father and mother while they made themselves as comfortable as they could on the hard floor.

Finally the storm broke in all its fury. The wind howled and shrieked. Lightning streaked the sky and thunders rolled along the cloudbanks. The rain came down so hard it began leaking in the house. Soon their bed was in a pool of water.

"Not a pleasant night," said the father. "I believe it is turning colder. I must keep the fire going." With that he got up and heaped the wood into the fireplace.

THE STRANGER'S GIFT

In very truth it had turned colder. When the rain stopped there came a chill that cut through the poor walls of their dwelling like a knife. All night long the aged couple huddled by the fire trying to keep warm and have enough heat, that their guest might be comfortable. With the first streak of dawn the mother began preparing breakfast.

"We have just enough flour for two cakes," she said, sadly. "I hope our guest will not think us stingy."

"We will give him what we have," said the father, "and if that does not seem enough, we can explain the situation."

Gretchen emptied the flour bin and made two rye cakes. Then she placed on the table the few scraps of meat that had been left from the evening meal. Now they called their guest. He came from the bedchamber looking refreshed and happy.

"I hope you had a comfortable night," said the father.

"Indeed I did," he replied. "I do not know how I will ever repay you for all your kindnesses to me."

"The good Lord has already repaid us many times, my friend," said the father. "Sit right up to the table and partake of our humble fare."

As the guest was about to sit down he asked, "May I say a blessing on the food?"

"That is our usual custom," answered the father.

WORLD OVER STORIES

All heads bowed as the guest offered his prayer. "Father, bless these thy children who have shown such kindness. We were homeless and they gave us shelter. We were hungry and they shared their last food with us. May the flour of their bin never fail and may they never know want."

After such a strange prayer the guest ate the food set before him and departed. The aged couple watched him as he passed down the path toward the road. Did their eyes deceive them? Did it not appear that the man was now clothed in a long white flowing robe? And was there a halo about his head?

Their interest in the stranger was soon dispelled by the coming of their son into the room.

"I'm hungry and I want lots to eat," called Johann in a gruff voice. "I suppose that beggar ate all there was left."

"Yes," said the mother. "We gave him the last of the flour."

"Why, here is meal enough for three cakes," said Johann, peering into the bin.

"What are you saying," cried the mother, in surprise. "I poured out all the flour when I made the cakes for our guest."

"Well, there is flour here now, anyhow," said the son. "Come and see for yourself."

The mother approached the bin timidly. Surely enough, there was flour enough for three full cakes. She prepared the food and they ate it thankfully.

THE STRANGER'S GIFT

"I want some more," called Johann when they had finished. "See if you can't scrape just a little bit more."

"No, my son, I used it all this time."

But Johann was not to be convinced. Again he approached the flour bin.

"You surely didn't. Here is enough meal for three cakes again. I want some more."

Now the father and mother looked at each other with something more than wonder in their eyes. Here indeed was a miracle.

"Did he not say, 'May the flour of the bin not fail, and may they not know want'?" spake the father in an awe-struck voice.

"Those were his words," replied the mother. "Those were his very words. Who could our guest have been?"

"We have entertained the Christ and knew it not," said the aged man. "And now his blessing rests upon us."

And thus it would seem. For from that day forth there was always enough meal in the bin for three cakes more. The aged couple had taken in the stranger and made him comfortable only to find that they had entertained the Christ unknowingly. Never again did they want for food.

THE BELOVED DISCIPLE

HE was a stalwart youth, that fisherman's lad, who lived on the shore of blue Galilee. He and his brother, James, spent their days in the synagogue school, but as soon as they were dismissed they rushed away to the lake, there to fish or swim or help their father's servants unload the boats.

Thus the boys grew to young manhood. When they were old enough their father permitted them to fish during the night. It was no uncommon thing for them to cast the net all night long. The boys loved to be out in God's nature, listening to the lapping of the water or looking at the brilliant stars above them.

"Who made the stars?" John would ask, musingly.

"The Scripture says, 'The heavens declare the glory of God,'" answered James.

Being of a serious turn of mind, they were greatly stirred when John the Baptist spoke his fiery messages along the Jordan River. They would have followed him gladly.

Then came the great event of their lives. Jesus of Nazareth came to their city teaching and healing the people. Thousands from all the countryside flocked to him, that they might hear his words and see his marvelous deeds. When one of

THE BELOVED DISCIPLE

the servants of their father was healed of his infirmity, their admiration knew no bounds.

"He is the One who will set up the kingdom," said John.

"And we should help him with his task," answered his brother.

One day, after teaching the people, Jesus wandered along the shore of the lake until he came to the fish shacks of their father. The two young men were in their boat mending nets as he passed by.

Looking at them with his piercing eyes, he said, "Follow me, and I will make you fishers of men." They left all and followed him.

Now this great leader gathered a band of twelve men about him that he might teach them. Month after month they went from place to place doing deeds of kindness.

On one occasion they were passing through a city and came to the leper colony on the outskirts. These poor people raised their usual cry, "Unclean, unclean!" But Jesus knew their need and healed them gladly.

Again they were in the city when Jairus, ruler of the synagogue, came to Jesus and begged him, saying, "My little daughter lieth at the point of death. I pray you come and heal her."

Jesus followed him to his home. Then taking the parents and three of his disciples, including our hero, he went in where the child was and said, "Little maiden, I say unto you, arise." And immediately she was restored to her parents.

WORLD OVER STORIES

Even John had many lessons to learn on these long tours. He was of a fiery temper and when things went wrong was wont to fly into a passion. Once, when entering a city of Samaria, the people were discourteous to Jesus.

"Call down fire upon their city," he cried, impetuously.

But Jesus answered: "John, John my beloved, you must control your temper. Your Scriptures say that you may hate your enemies. But I say unto you, Love your enemies, and pray for them which persecute you, that ye may be the children of your Father who is in heaven."

By such deeds and such teachings did Jesus prepare them for the work that lay before them.

Then came the time of the Passover Feast at Jerusalem. For three years Jesus had been teaching in their cities and synagogues. They presumed that soon he would set up his earthly kingdom in Jerusalem.

But this was to be a time of great disappointment for them. There came that day of triumph when Jesus rode into the city amid the shouts of the people.

"Hosannah to the Son of David, blessed is he that cometh in the name of the Lord! Hosannah in the highest!" came the exultant cries of the multitude.

Within a week, however, their leader was taken by the soldiers while in the garden, Gethsemane, and after a mock trial was crucified.

It was now that John and the other disciples

THE BELOVED DISCIPLE

must learn to follow the teachings of the leader without his presence. They shortly established a church in Jerusalem. James and John were among its foremost leaders. In fact, so zealous was John for the cause of Christ that the Romans finally banished him to the lonely island, Patmos. Here he wrote the words of cheer and comfort recorded in the last book of the Bible.

When he was released, this faithful worker settled in the city of Ephesus. He who had been so strong-tempered as a youth had now learned Christ's ideal of loving his enemies. By his generous and kindly life he built up a large community of Christians.

John, the beloved disciple, lived to ripe old age. Tradition says that he was at Ephesus when he reached his hundredth birthday. His friends tenderly carried him to the church, that he might speak to them. Raising himself on his elbow he uttered the single sentence, "Little children, love one another." They asked him if he had anything further to say and he added, "Little children, love one another."

Suddenly there was great confusion in the rear of the church. The cry of "Roman soldiers" rang through the room.

They rushed within. Seeing the aged leader they carried him without the building, tied him to a chariot, and dragged him about the city until he was dead.

The beloved disciple became a martyr for the cause of Christ.

THE GAMIN OF PARIS

LITTLE GAVROCHE, the street urchin of Paris, stood before a shop window where tempting foods were on display. He was trying to decide when he had last eaten a meal.

"Brr-r-r, it's cold. Let me see. Was it Tuesday or Wednesday? Brr-r-r. Well, whenever it was, this is Friday, and I know I'm hungry."

A strange sight he made, this pinched, weazened little lad of eight years. His long, tangled hair stuck out from beneath a cast-off cap. His trousers, formerly worn by some adult, were now an array of rags hung together in a manner known only to himself. About his neck was a shawl which he had picked up in some alley, that helped to keep his shoulders warm although the rest of his small body shivered in the damp evening air.

"Yes, sir, it's time this gentleman dines. But where are the pennies to buy this meal?"

Just then Gavroche noticed two other children pass by the window. They were well dressed as compared with his rags. From their general attitude they seemed to be in trouble. Timidly they approached a barber shop next door and entered. A moment later they were thrust

THE GAMIN OF PARIS

violently out into the street. The smaller one began to cry.

"What's the matter, young 'uns?" asked Gavroche, as he came up beside them.

"We don't know where our parents are and we have no place to sleep," answered the older boy, a lad of seven.

A feeling of sympathy swept through the heart of the little urchin. Here were two children like himself, waifs in a large city. Unlike him, they did not know how to care for themselves, while he had been obliged to make his own way for years. Gavroche felt a great desire to help them in their distress.

"Aw, that's all right," he said, in a gruff, offhand sort of way. "Don't cry about that. You just come with me. I'll show you a fine place where you can sleep like young princes."

The smaller children were truly grateful for their new-found friend. Together they turned down the street, Rue Saint Antoine, leading toward the Bastille.

As they rounded a corner the smaller children had an opportunity to see of what stuff their new companion was made. There, under a doorway, sat a little beggar girl trying to sleep. Her clothes were much too thin for the piercing air, and she was numb with cold.

"Poor child," muttered Gavroche. "She'll get sick if she doesn't take better care of herself." With that he unwound the scarf from his neck and flung it over her shoulders. With a loud

WORLD OVER STORIES

"Brrr-r-r" he started down the street again in the foggy night.

"By the way, young 'uns, have you had supper?" he suddenly asked.

"We haven't had a bite to eat since morning," whimpered the younger child.

"Time to eat," he said, grandly, smiling within as he remembered his own three-day fast. "Time to eat. Come right this way, gentlemen."

He began fumbling in all the nooks and crannies of his tattered garments as they strode toward a cheap shop. Triumphantly at last he drew forth a sou.

"Here is supper for three," he shouted, pushing open the door of the baker's shop.

"Three pieces of bread," he commanded mannishly, laying his sou on the counter. The baker took out a black loaf and prepared to cut the slices.

"White bread, I want," he said, loudly, noticing the mistake.

The baker took out a large loaf of white bread and cut off three generous slices. Gavroche gave the two larger slices to the children and munched away at the smaller one. When they had eaten it to the last crumb they fared forth into the night again.

The sleeping quarters of little Gavroche were a strange place indeed. Years before, Napoleon had started a monument to be built in memory of himself as Commander-in-Chief of the Army of Egypt. This monument took the form of an

THE GAMIN OF PARIS

elephant, forty feet high, and made of masonry and timbers. For some reason it had never been completed. Some novice painter had given it a coat of green paint, but the wind and weather had stained it black. Here it stood in the corner of a little park, a lonely, crumbling phantom in a sleeping city.

The lad led his guests to this strange colossus.

"This is our distinguished guest chamber," he said, pointing upward to a dark hole between the forelegs. "But first let me get the ladder." Making his way toward the fence, he drew forth a ladder from the grass. It reached only part way to the black darkness of the hole.

"You go first, my friends," he said. But his little guests seemed afraid to trust themselves to the darkness above. Seeing their hesitancy he sprang up the ladder and swung himself easily within the elephant.

"Now you climb up and I will help you," he said. By constant urging and much effort he got the two children safely into his nook.

Gavroche now dug out a piece of tape he kept near the entrance. Lighting it he led the way with this flickering candle toward a mattress of straw and a gray woolen blanket that was inclosed in a tentlike screen.

"Time to sleep," he said, showing them his bed.

"Why do you have the tent over it?" asked the younger child, innocently.

"That is to keep off the rats and mice that come to visit me," he answered, gayly. "But

WORLD OVER STORIES

don't you worry. When we get inside and get the edges down they can never find you."

Within a few moments the three children were safely tucked under the quilt. But scarcely had the light gone out than strange noises were heard. The children began to whimper.

"Never you mind that," said Gavroche, reassuringly. "Nothing can hurt you here. Catch hold of my hand and close your eyes."

Soon the three homeless children were fast asleep, safe from the wind and the rain. And happiest of that group was the little gamin of the streets whose deed of kindness had brought joy to those less fortunate than himself.

(Adapted from *Les Misérables*,
by Victor Hugo.)

SIR GALAHAD

ENCHANTED castles, stirring adventures in the forest, tournaments, knights in full armor hurled to the ground biting the dirt, the loud clash of battle, gay laugh of ladies, Court of King Arthur and his valiant men.

Such is the setting of the story of Sir Galahad. Born in bonnie England many years ago, he was brought up in an Abbey on the edge of the dark forest not far from the fabled city of Camelot. As a youth he loved to roam the forest, practicing with his bow and arrow or searching out the secrets of the wee, wild things of the forest.

As he grew to young manhood he was taught by the knights to wield the heavy battle-ax and to hurl the javelin. The ladies of the Abbey taught him in the ways of chivalry and courtesy and honor.

When he met some difficult task he would say: "I must conquer this task. Some day I will be a member of the Round Table, and only brave men are allowed there."

When he was tempted to do a wrong deed, he would say: "I must never stoop to evil. Only the pure and noble are worthy of being knights. I must keep my heart pure."

Thus the youth came to manhood strong of arm and courageous of heart.

It was on the eve of Pentecost, when Galahad was nearing his eighteenth birthday, that our story begins. He had spent the day in the forest hunting and now approached the Abbey as the twilight gathered. He had been thinking of the time when he should be dubbed "knight" and would go in quest of adventure.

"The time will soon come," he mused. "I am now old enough and have proved my ability with the sword and the bow. Soon I can strike out toward Camelot and mingle with the knights of the Round Table."

As Galahad came out of the forest he saw a horseman approaching. Out of a cloud of dust emerged the famous knight, Lancelot, and made his way into the Abbey.

"My time is come," said Galahad with glad heart. "Soon I will be knighted."

And so it proved. Scarcely had he entered the Abbey when one of the ladies came to him and spoke as follows.

"Prepare yourself, my Galahad, to spend the night in prayer in the chapel. To-morrow, with the rising of the sun, you will be knighted."

The youth now quickly put on a flowing red robe, the emblem of purity, and entered into the dimly lighted chapel. Through the long hours of the night, beside the flickering candles, he knelt at the altar in prayer, asking for purity of life and the ability to do helpful deeds to all persons in need. When the sun's first beams streaked in through the window, a company of knights and

SIR GALAHAD

ladies entered the chapel. Sir Lancelot approached the altar and spoke to the youth.

"You are now to be made a knight, a member of the Court of our beloved King Arthur. You know the vows of knighthood. Do you swear to ever help the weak and helpless, never to leave a friend, and to live nobly before your king and your God?"

"I do," said Galahad, humbly.

"Then in the name of King Arthur I dub thee knight," said Lancelot. "Let spurs, sword and shield be given to him."

Sir Lancelot himself bound on the spurs while the ladies decked him with pennant and ribbons, sword and shield. The youth was now fully clad to go forth to brave deeds.

Meanwhile, in the city of Camelot, the king and his court were assembling for the time of celebration that accompanied Pentecost. It was the custom to spend the morning in religious ceremonies and to follow this with a great banquet. At the table each knight had his particular place. At the head of the table sat the king, and beside him was a chair, a strange and marvelous chair, upon which only the pure and noble knight dared sit. If any other person presumed to sit in it, he was pitched out headlong. Even more grave misfortune might befall him for his impudence.

On this particular day the king and his nobles had already assembled and the feast was begun. The chair, as usual, was empty. Now Sir Galahad entered the room. An aged man clothed in pure white at once came forward and took him by the hand. Before the astonished gaze of every member present Galahad was led straight to the Perilous Seat beside the king and seated there. No harm of any kind came to him.

"This is indeed the pure knight, long foretold in our history, who shall do marvelous things for us," said the king to himself. Then, addressing the youthful Galahad, he said, "We welcome you to our goodly company, young sir, and hope that your whole life may prove an example for us all."

This was Sir Galahad's introduction to the court.

It was the custom, at this early day in England, for the knights of the Round Table to go each year in search of the Holy Grail. This was the cup from which the Christ drank on the night of the Last Supper. It had first been given to Joseph of Arimathæa, the one who furnished a tomb for the Christ at his burial. When Joseph finally died, it had mysteriously disappeared, only to reappear again in that country where brave men and pure were worthy of possessing it. The nobles of the court were, even now, preparing to go forth in quest of it. Sir Galahad planned to go with them.

Again a night was spent in prayer. Now the large company of knights waited in silence in the chapel while a blessing was said over them. Then, with streaming pennants, they rode forth into all lands in search of the Grail.

SIR GALAHAD

Space will not permit to tell of all the gallant deeds done by Sir Galahad. On one occasion he emerged from a dark forest to find a castle guarded by seven powerful knights. These base men had terrorized the countryside for years, killing any who displeased them and carrying off fair maidens to be held for ransom.

Single-handed and alone Galahad rode forward to give battle. Again and again he charged them, striking and parrying, dashing and swirling, unhorsing a man here, delivering a crashing blow there. After hours of combat he came off victor. Then he rode boldly into the castle and freed all those who were imprisoned. Great was the rejoicing of the countryside to know that their ancient enemies were destroyed.

On another occasion he came to the castle of King Amfortas. This man and his entire court were under a wicked spell so that no person could move from the spot where he stood. A demon had cast the spell and stood guard in the courtyard. It was reported that only a pure knight would have a chance in destroying the demon and breaking the charm.

Galahad's pure life gave him confidence that he could win in the conflict. Riding up the drawbridge, he attacked the monster who guarded its gate. This huge animal seemed to send out flames of fire from its nostrils. His horse was quickly killed by the demon. Now he must fight on foot. But Galahad bravely charged the beast and dealt blow after blow. For hours he fought, sometimes seeming to be defeated, then again gaining ground. At last, with one fell thrust, he brought the monster to the ground, dead.

Now the spell was broken. King Amfortas rose from his couch and with the members of his household came forward to thank their deliverer for his courageous deed.

Finally, after years of wandering in foreign lands, Galahad decided to return to his own home. As he approached the shore of the ocean that separated England from France his path led by a little chapel in the woods. An old man sat before the door, the aged man whom Galahad recognized as the one who had led him to the Seat Perilous in Arthur's banquet hall.

"Come," said the aged Roger. "I have waited long for you. You are the one to whom is intrusted the Holy Grail. Follow me within."

Together they entered the chapel. As Galahad's eyes became accustomed to the darkness he seemed to see a glimmer of light in a far corner. It was as though a lamp were covered with a piece of crimson cloth.

Now the light came nearer. Invisible hands were bringing it toward him. The rays from the lamp became more blinding. Finally it rested even within his own grasp. A voice, calm and clear, spoke out of the darkness, saying,

"To you, O pure of heart, to you is intrusted this priceless boon. May you enjoy its blessings so long as life shall last. Indeed, blessed are the pure in heart." Sir Galahad had found the Grail.

PAULUS THE COBBLER

IN the city of Tiberius there once lived an old cobbler by the name of Paulus. Although he had reached the age of ninety, each day one could hear the rap-a-tap-tap of his hammer mending the shoes of his customers.

Paulus came to be known throughout the entire city as a fine cobbler and a most kind-hearted man. He always did more work on each pair of shoes than was required, he used the best of materials, and he never overcharged a customer.

But aside from his work as a shoemaker he was best known and loved for his generous deeds. His father had given to him a small plot of land planted to fig trees. It was his custom to gather a basket of figs each day, during the bearing season, and take them to some sick person or shut-in. Offering his gift and speaking a word of cheer, he would return to his home happy.

"Who is the kindest man in this city?" the Emperor asked one day.

"Paulus the cobbler," answered one of his nobles.

"And who is Paulus the cobbler?"

"An aged man who lives on the street Claudia," said the courtier.

"I must know such a man," said the Emperor. So saying he called for his chariot and commanded the driver to take him to the home of Paulus. Reaching the place he found the aged cobbler planting a fig tree.

"Thou art Paulus the cobbler," spake the Emperor, entering the yard. "I have heard much of thee."

"Such is my name," answered the old man, simply.

"Wherefore dost thou plant this fig tree?" asked the Emperor.

"That I may bear the ripe figs to my friends and thus do my daily deed of kindness," said Paulus. "With God's good pleasure I may still partake of the fruit of this tree."

"Tell me thine age," said the Emperor.

"I have lived in this city ninety years," replied the old man.

"Ninety years and still expect to eat of the fruit of this tree?" cried the Emperor.

"If such be God's will," the shoemaker replied.

"Well," spake the Emperor, "if thou dost live until ripe figs are on this tree, I pray thee share them with me."

"That I will gladly," said Paulus.

Thereupon the Emperor turned to his chariot and was driven away.

More years sped by. Paulus spent his days working over his last or spading among his trees. Each day he filled his basket with figs and distributed them among the poor. When he reached his hundredth birthday the fig tree he last planted bore luscious fruit.

PAULUS THE COBBLER

"I will take the most choice fruit of this tree to the Emperor," thought Paulus.

Thereupon he filled his small basket and proceeded on his errand. At the palace gate he told the guard of his purpose and was admitted to the presence of the Emperor.

"What is thy wish?" asked the Emperor, not recognizing his friend.

"Lo, I am the old man to whom thou didst say, on seeing him planting a fig tree, 'If thou livest to eat of the fruit, share it with me,' and behold, I have come and brought thee of the fruit, that thou mayest partake of it likewise."

The Emperor was much pleased with the gift of the aged man. Emptying the basket he filled it with gold coins.

"I have heard of thy kindly deeds to the poor. This, Paulus, is but a just reward for thy helpfulness. If ever thou art in need, I pray thee let me know."

"I am in God's hands," humbly replied the cobbler. Then thanking the Emperor for his generosity he hobbled away home.

Next door to this old man there lived a woman whose stingy habits and harsh tongue made her disliked by all her neighbors. When she heard of Paulus' good fortune she called her husband and desired him to try his luck. Filling an immense basket with figs she bade him carry it to the Emperor.

"He filled Paulus' basket with gold; perchance he will fill thine likewise."

WORLD OVER STORIES

When her husband approached the gate of the palace, he told his errand to the guard, saying, "I brought these figs to the Emperor. Empty my basket, I pray thee, and fill it up with gold again."

The guard hastened away to the throne room to bear his message. When the Emperor heard this stupid request he laughed long and loud.

"Set his basket in the hallway of the palace," he commanded, "and order the man to stand ten paces from it. Place a sign that all who pass are to pelt him with his figs."

The remainder of that afternoon the foolish husband ducked and dodged the figs that were hurled at him. At night he returned home to his wife, wounded and crestfallen.

He received slight sympathy from her.

"Never mind," she said, "thou hast one comfort. Had they been cocoanuts instead of figs thou mightest have suffered harder raps."

(Adapted from the Talmud.)

A KING IN RAGS AND A BEGGAR ON THE THRONE

THE scene of our story is laid in the dank dungeon cell of King Herod's palace. Here John the Baptist, forerunner of the Christ and mighty champion of the coming Kingdom, sat upon the cold stone bench awaiting his fate. It was two months since he had been thrust into this place. He, the king at heart, had come before Herod, that beggar on the throne, and confronted him with his evil deeds. For that crime, if crime it was, he had been imprisoned.

"It must be late in the afternoon," mused the man, watching the slanting rays of the sun as they filtered through the hole in the massive wall high above.

Suddenly a picture rose before him.

He was again a boy, in his Judæan home. He was about to go with his father to offer incense in the Temple. Together they mounted the Temple steps. He heard the chanting of the people and the choir as they sang the songs of David. He saw the smoke of incense mount heavenward. He heard the priest's deep-toned voice saying,

"O Lord, bless thy people, and forget not thine heritage."

"So let it be," answered the multitude.

WORLD OVER STORIES

But the vision changed, and he thought of his days in the wilderness of Judæa, of his preaching to the people, of the events which led to his imprisonment. John loved to be out in God's nature world. The flower in the crannied rocks, the wild, glad, joyous song of the birds, the beasts that stalked the mountains all told of the wonder and glory of God.

Day after day he lived in these quiet places talking with his Maker. His cloak was made of camel's hair and his food was that common to the wilderness—locusts and wild honey. He dreamed of the time when his people and nation should again be the great people they had been in the past.

But as John mingled with others he saw the injustice that was going on. The poor were oppressed. The rich lived in revelry and sin. He felt that God would punish them for their wrongdoing.

"Repent, repent," he thundered, shaking his dark, shaggy locks, "for the kingdom of heaven is at hand."

His striking appearance and unusual words drew thousands to the bank of the Jordan River to see and hear him. They thought that another of the ancient prophets had returned to Israel.

When the common people asked what they should do, he taught them the lesson of helpfulness.

"He that hath two coats, let him give to him that hath none."

A KING IN RAGS

Then came the publicans asking what they should do.

"Stop your thieving," he said, boldly; "exact no more than that which is appointed."

To the soldiers, rough, uncouth men, he said, "Do violence to no man, neither accuse any falsely."

Such fearless preaching caused his fame to spread far and wide. He baptized thousands in the waters of the Jordan.

Then, upon a certain day, this courageous champion of right was confronted with the greatest test of his life. He had heard much of the wicked life of King Herod; how that monarch set an example of sinfulness for his people. No man dared accuse the king of his bad deeds. To do so would probably cost that man his life.

Here was a real challenge to John. Should he continue working among the common people or should he go straight to the leader and tell him of his evil deeds?

John never hesitated, even for a minute, to do what he thought was right. King at heart, he entered the palace of Herod and soon stood before that craven. Raising his arm and pointing directly at the king, he said: "You are a sinful man. You are setting a bad example for your people. Repent and change your ways or God will punish you."

Under ordinary circumstances such an accusation would have brought instant death. But Herod seemed to take a fancy to this youth who

WORLD OVER STORIES

was courageous enough to challenge him with his wrongdoings. He was about to let him go.

But Herodias, the queen, had heard John's words, and their stinging rebuke cut her to the quick. She became furious at this bold champion and had him cast into prison. Then she awaited the time of her revenge. That time was not far distant.

It so happened that the king had a birthday not long afterward and prepared a great banquet for himself and his nobles. It was to be a time of unusual rejoicing. The banquet hall was gorgeously bedecked with flowers, while the tables groaned under their load of delicate fruits and viands.

Finally all the guests arrived and the festivities began. Flagons of wine were filled again and again. The queen now sat in a side room, watching, waiting, for the moment of her revenge to arrive.

Then the king rose and in a drunken stupor called for his little daughter, Salome, to come and entertain them. The child came out and danced the strange Oriental dance, so much admired by the nobles.

"Huzzah! Huzzah!" shouted the nobles at its close.

"Ask what you will," said the king, calling her back, "ask what you will, even to the half of my kingdom, and it shall be given you."

The child stepped into the room where her mother was sitting.

A KING IN RAGS

"What boon should I ask of the king?" said the child to her mother.

"Go to your father," said the queen, "and demand the head of John the Baptist."

Herod was rudely shaken from his drunkenness by this demand. He admired John greatly and would have let him go. But, because of his promise, he commanded soldiers to carry out the request.

Suddenly John was aroused from his musings by the tread of soldier feet in the passageway. A key turned in the door. They entered his cell.

"Your life is demanded by the king," said the leader, coming before him.

Now, this true nobleman showed his courage. Raising his eyes for a moment in prayer he went to death a martyr to the cause of right and righteousness.

Of such stuff are heroes made.

A CHAMPION OF THE POOR

LORD SHAFTESBURY was comfortably seated by the fireplace in the palatial home of his uncle. It was a bleak Christmas Eve. Without, the wind howled round the corners and whistled down the chimney flue. Within all was light and warmth and comfort. The man sat watching the logs burn away.

"A penny for your thoughts, noble Lord," shouted a gay young lady, coming close to his chair.

"I was just thinking how many would not have a happy Christmas this year," said Shaftesbury, thoughtfully.

"For shame, for shame, to spoil so happy a party by such sad thoughts," she cried. Again the shouts of merry laughter filled the room.

As the hour of ten struck Lord Shaftesbury rose and made ready to depart.

"What? Not going so soon," said his uncle, noting his intentions. "Our party has just begun."

"If you will pardon me, uncle, I should like to be excused," he replied.

Lord Shaftesbury hastened from the comfortable home of his uncle and started toward the bridge over the Thames. On the way he bought a lantern. Now he began hunting among the

A CHAMPION OF THE POOR

sheltered crannies under the bridge where people were accustomed to spend the night. Within an hour he had forty or fifty persons. He took them home to his own house and provided a bed for each one that night. On this evening he began a custom that he continued till the end of his life.

Who was this man, this champion of the poor? His name was Anthony A. Cooper, although he is more commonly known as Lord Shaftesbury. He had been brought up in a home of wealth, but could not live content that others should suffer. When he became a Member of Parliament he started many laws that would better the conditions of the poor.

His first law was for a shorter working day for the common laborer. He had seen these men shuffle home after fourteen hours of labor, completely worn out. He felt that they deserved a better wage and shorter working hours.

In studying the conditions of the poor he made frequent trips to the slums. His heart was filled with pity as he saw the places where people must live. The houses were vile holes of filth and dirt. Families lived underground in one or two rooms. There was little light or ventilation in their homes. Sometimes two, or even three families lived in a single room. Disease spread rapidly in such conditions. Worst of all, the little children were taught to be criminals by those who lived in these slums quarters.

Shaftesbury began a regular struggle in **Parliament** for laws to improve housing conditions.

WORLD OVER STORIES

Soon he had these foul houses torn down. Other buildings were erected in their place that would give plenty of light and air. These must be kept clean. They were to be whitewashed every six months. Grass and trees began to grow where formerly was filth. His constant labors soon made the East End of London a place of beauty, compared to what it had formerly been.

His attention was now turned to the coal miners. The grasping mine owners were laying off their men and hiring women and children to work in the pits. Shaftesbury made many trips to see conditions for himself. Then he put forward a law that would forbid child and woman workers in the mines.

On many occasions he had noticed that the children of the streets were not receiving any education. This made him most sorrowful. He began asking how schools might be erected for them. No money was to be had. One day he heard of a poor cobbler who gathered the children about him and taught them while he worked. This gave Shaftesbury an idea. He began searching out persons who would be willing to teach in this way. The wealthy people of the city often scoffed at his "Ragged Schools," as they were called, and would not give for their support. But this courageous man went right on without them. Within a few years ten thousand children had been taught in his day schools, night schools and Sunday-school classes.

"Paper, mister, paper?" came the small piping

A CHAMPION OF THE POOR

voice of a child one cold winter night. Shaftesbury bought a paper just to help the child. The little fellow's fingers were so cold he dropped his money in making change. The noble Lord thought of a plan for helping the newspaper boys. He would loan them ten dollars apiece with which they could build a small shelter on the street corner. He helped them plan the shelters and saw that they were properly made. He thought that he would probably give away a thousand dollars or more in this scheme. But, strange to relate, every lad returned the money to him as soon as his earnings permitted. For this bit of kindness to the newsboys Shaftesbury lost scarcely a penny.

For fifty years our hero was one of the busiest men in all England. During this time he was a member of Parliament. Twice he was a Cabinet member. He headed many committees that were working for the betterment of the laboring classes. In very truth he wore his life out in bringing comfort to others. He built a home for boys who had just come to the city for the first time. He founded a home for women. He loaned money to the match girls, also, for shelters in the winter time. He formed a loan association for fathers out of work in the winter. A thousand women received ten dollars apiece to build coffee or sandwich stands on the street corners. Such was the life of the noble Lord Shaftesbury.

At his death thousands of persons, the rich

from their homes of luxury and the poor from their homes of poverty, came to look a last time at the face of this true nobleman. He had given of his life to help others. He had left the world a happier place than he had found it.

THE KING WHO LEARNED KINDNESS

THERE was once a king who was a mighty hunter. He lived in a large palace and his servants each day brought him choice foods and rare wines. The food he liked best was the flesh of the deer. Scarcely a day passed in which he did not have venison for his meat.

But the king grew tired of the long rides in quest of game. He began wondering how he could shoot the deer without spending so much effort in finding them.

"I have a plan," spoke one of his nobles. "When you would go hunting, O king, let the people of the village go into the forest and drive the deer into the deep valley over beyond the palace. You need only to go there and shoot them as they pass."

This wise advice greatly pleased the king. He made such a decree. From that day forth the people of the villages must leave their work and by forming a huge circle in the forest drive the deer into the proper place. Although the plan worked well for the king the people soon began to complain.

"How can we do our work," they cried, "when the king would keep us in the forest almost every day of the summer?"

Then one of their leaders came forward with a remedy. They would gain the king's consent to make the valley into a large park surrounded by high walls. Then they would drive the deer within the park.

"We can go on with our work and the king can hunt whenever he chooses," concluded the man. The king quickly gave his consent to the new plan; the park was made and the deer were driven within.

It so happened that the deer who came within the park were of two separate herds, the Banyan deer and the Monkey deer. Each herd had its own king. The king of the Banyan herd was a fine, strong fellow with a coat the color of gold, and wide, spreading antlers. The king of the Monkey herd was darker in color but equally strong and well-built. They stood near the gate of the park as the great king came by.

"Are you the leaders of these two herds?" he asked.

"We are," they answered.

"Your lives shall be spared," said the king. "I will instruct my servants that they shall never shoot at you." Thus these two leaders were free from danger.

But the other members of the herds did not fare so well. Those who were sent by the king to do his hunting were careless fellows who wounded many a deer and left him to suffer.

Now the leader of the Banyan deer spoke to the king of the Monkey deer, saying: "We must

KING WHO LEARNED KINDNESS

do something to save our herds. Many are being needlessly wounded. I suggest that on one day a member of my herd go up to be killed and that on the next one of your herd go. This will prevent needless injury."

The plan seemed so much better than the way things were going that it was quickly put into effect. When the king's cook came to the park each day he found, first one of the Banyan deer, then one of the Monkey deer waiting for him.

One day it was the turn of the Monkey deer to choose a member. This was done by lot. It so happened that the lot fell on a mother deer who had a little yellow fawn. The mother came before the king of the Monkey deer, saying: "O king, the lot has fallen on me. But if I die, what will happen to my baby? Only let me go for now until my little one is older; then I will give myself up to be killed."

The king listened to her request, then said: "I cannot help you. The lot has fallen on you. It is your turn to die. Your little fawn must get along as best it can without you."

Now the mother deer hastened to the king of the Banyan herd and told him her troubles.

"Go back to your baby," he said, kindly. "I will see that your place is filled."

Imagine the surprise of the cook that morning to find the king of the Banyan deer with his head on the block when that man came to the park for his master's meat. Since he had been told not to harm the leaders of either herd, he went

WORLD OVER STORIES

back to the palace to ask the Great King what should be done.

"I will go to the park and find out about this," said the king after hearing the words of his cook.

"Leader of the Banyan herd," he said, coming to the entrance of the park, "why are you here? I promised you your life, and here you are with your head on the block. What does it mean?"

"O great king, I thank you for your promise of safety," said the king of the Banyans. "But this morning there came to me a mother with a little baby, saying that the lot had fallen on her. She did not wish to die until her little one was old enough to care for itself. I could not ask anyone else to take her place, so I have come myself."

"Most noble deer," said the great king, "never before have I seen such kindness, nay, not among men. You shame me. Go in safety. Not only do I grant you your life but I will no longer kill the deer in the forest."

From thenceforth the deer were freed from the park and were no longer harmed by the king or his servants.

(Adapted from the JATAKA.)

JOAN OF ARC

"A STORY, a story, Miss Carson!" cried the girls, crowding about their leader. "A story before we close our club to-day!"

Miss Carson paused a moment.

"Very well, girls," she said, "I will tell you of a most interesting side trip I took last summer while visiting in France. I am going to tell you about the heroine of the French people. Can anyone tell me her name?"

"Joan of Arc," ventured one of the girls.

"You are right. Now can anyone possibly guess when she lived?"

"I think she was killed some time about 1400," said Edith, the assistant group leader.

"That is a very good guess," said Miss Carson. "Now listen and I will tell you the story of her life.

"It was about 1410 that a little girl was born into a peasant home in Domrémy, a little village in Louraine. Her parents, Jacques and Isabeau d'Arc, were pious and devout people who trained their daughter in the ways of right.

"Joan grew up to be a charming child. She was full of life and vigor, happy and smiling at all times. Before she was as old as most of you she had made a name for herself in her village because of her gentleness and kindness to the sick and suffering.

"Being a peasant child, she often had to tend the sheep on the hillside. This she loved best of all, for it allowed her to be out among the birds and bees and flowers. But her little fingers were not always idle. She became one of the most skilled needlewomen in all that country round.

"There was one place, not far from her home, where Joan loved to go. It was a little village chapel. Hard beside it grew an old and renowned beech tree, with great and beautiful arms, with a rich foliage which protected the weary visitor who sat at its feet from the rays of the sun. Joan's godmother had told her that this tree was the home of the fairies. Joan felt sure that she could hear the fairy music when she sat in its branches.

"But some things brought sorrow to the heart of this simple peasant maid. Her country, her beloved France, was fast being overrun by the English. The dauphin (uncrowned king of France) was being worsted constantly by the British troopers. City after city fell. Army after army was defeated. Each added loss came like a heart stab to this sensitive child. Something must be done and at once.

"It was when she was about thirteen years of age that there seemed to come a vision from heaven to her, telling her that some day she should set France free. At first the child was surprised at such thoughts. But as these visions

JOAN OF ARC

came oftener and became more real she finally decided that they must be true.

"Joan did not dare tell her parents about these strange messages. Her father had vowed that he would rather kill her with his own hands than have her follow the rude men of the army.

"Yet she felt that she must do something for her downtrodden country and king. Finally she appealed to the governor of her province. He scoffed at her foolish notions. If the trained leaders of the army could not win battles, surely a simple peasant girl could not.

"However, Joan did not give up. Again and again for days and weeks she appealed to him that he take her to the king. Although he did not, other important persons heard her story and believed in her.

"It was about 1428 that Joan of Arc was finally able to gain an audience with the king. He had no faith in her so-called visions and messages. He attempted to fool her. When she entered his throne room he dressed up as one of the nobles and allowed another to sit on his throne. But Joan was not to be fooled by this ruse. She walked straight to him and said: 'Most noble Lord Dauphin, I am Joan, the maid sent on behalf of God to aid you and your kingdom; and by his command I announce to you that you shall be crowned in the city of Rheims, and shall become his lieutenant in the realm of France.'

"The common people and the soldiers heard the strange words of Joan. Although there seemed no possible hope of her words coming true, they had confidence in her.

"Finally the king gathered an army of some five thousand to send to the besieged city of Orleans. These people were hemmed in on all sides by the English and their food supply was fast giving out. Unless help came soon they must surrender.

"Joan fitted herself out for this conflict. She had a coat-of-mail made for herself. She sewed a beautiful white flag upon which were the fleurs-de-lis of France and the figure of the Christ. Then, finding the sword said to have been used by Charles Martel in his fight against the Saracens, she sallied forth.

"Before going she did still another thing. She wrote a letter to the English general announcing her mission from on high, and demanding that he withdraw from France. Although the English generals paid little attention to this letter, the common soldiers began to fear her. She seemed to be a supernatural power that was come to fight against them.

"Then, one dark night, mid the clash and roll of the thunder, her little army marched straight into the fortress of Orleans without any opposition from the enemy.

"What great rejoicing this caused in France! Joan's first promise had already been accomplished. Within a few weeks the British were entirely driven from their strongholds about the city.

JOAN OF ARC

"Now Joan returned to the king. It was time he be crowned in Rheims as rightful ruler of the land.

" 'Noble Lord Dauphin,' she cried, 'I am told to go forward. Come, rouse yourself, noble sir. We must on to Rheims.'

"However, Charles was not sure of her plans. Fortified cities held by the enemy lay between his comfortable palace and the city of Rheims. Even Rheims itself was in the control of the British. What guarantee of success had he with his poorly equipped troops?

" 'Forward, forward, my friends. The Lord has delivered them into our hands,' was her constant cry.

"When the common people were at length won over to her side the king had to give in. Taking a large army and his best generals, he ventured forth.

"The fact that Joan of Arc rode at the head of her troopers struck terror into the hearts of the English soldiers. Town after town was given up without a struggle. Then, on July 16, the king made his triumphal entry into Rheims. The following day, in the grand cathedral, the gentle Dauphin was crowned with the circlet of gold that had rested on the heads of his ancestors, as king of France.

"Joan had now completed her task. She had freed Orleans and seen the king crowned in Rheims. She desired to return to her home in Domrémy. But the selfish nobles would not

WORLD OVER STORIES

consider it for a minute. Her presence was of too much value in controlling the soldiers.

"Again Joan donned her coat-of-mail and went into Normandy to fight against the enemy. Still later we find her in defense of Compiègne.

"Then came the sad, bitter end. While gallantly fighting, one day she was captured. She was accused of being a witch and sentenced to die.

"On the 30th day of May, 1431, a high platform was built in the market place of Rouen. At noontime a guard of eight hundred spearsmen escorted this nineteen-year-old heroine to her place of martyrdom. With a prayer on her lips for her persecutors she died as bravely as she had lived.

"Joan of Arc died for her country," concluded Miss Carson. "We are permitted to live for ours. May we be as true and loyal as she."

THE SONG OF THE SHEPHERD KING

KING DAVID sat in his palace in the city of Jerusalem. It was sunset on a warm autumn day. The purple haze hung over the olive trees and ragged walls of the distant mountain. How strangely familiar that deep valley in the mountains looked!

Now a picture rose in the mind of the old man. He was no longer a king in his palace. He was a lad again in the village of Bethlehem. It was an early summer morning.

"Come, my son," called his father. "You must hasten with your sheep. The pasture is growing scarce and you will have to travel far. Get your flocks going before it grows too hot."

"Coming, father," shouted the lad, scrambling out of bed.

He was soon in the common room of their humble dwelling.

"How did things go yesterday?" asked the father.

David hesitated. "A lion got the old ewe," finally said the youth with downcast looks. Such a thing was a disgrace to any shepherd.

"That is bad," said his father. "You must practice with your sling."

After a hasty breakfast David set out for the

sheepfold. The welcome "ba-ba-ing" of his sheep told him that they were ready to be going.

"The most verdant pastures lie beyond the valley in the fields of Boaz," thought the lad.

Sounding his call, he turned his flock toward this spot. It was a dangerous road that he was choosing. The dark shadows shrouded the rugged valley and here the wild beasts lurked. There was the constant danger also that one of his flock would be crowded off the rocky ledge to the depths below.

"I must have my sling ready," he said, unwinding the leathern thongs. "If any animal shows up this time, I will try to give a good account of myself."

One should not think that this youth was unskilled with the sling. For days at a time, while his sheep nibbled the grass, he had stood in the dry river-bed throwing the round pebbles at a distant target. Each day he had grown more accurate in aim and more strong of arm. The lion on the previous day had taken him quite by surprise.

"Let him try it again," said the lad, almost wishing the beast would come out of his lair.

Hardly had he entered the deep chasm that separated him from the pasture lands when his troubles began. He heard a piteous bleating behind him.

"That little lamb will try to crowd by," he muttered, hastening back.

Sure enough, there was a little lamb that had

SONG OF THE SHEPHERD KING

fallen part way down the steep cliff. David leaned far over with his shepherd's crook and drew the lamb back to safety. Catching it up in his arm he started on.

"You will have to walk by yourself," he said, gently, stroking its woolly head. "I must be ready with my sling."

Now the sheep were approaching the bottom of the valley. The shepherd quickened his pace. Then suddenly he heard a loud roar. Above him on a ledge crouched a lion, about to spring.

His sling whirred above his head. Then one of the strings loosened from his hand, and the stone whizzed through the air. There came another roar, but this time it was one of pain. The animal rolled over on the ground—dead.

"I think you are through," he said, preparing his sling for another emergency. "You did your work yesterday; I do mine to-day."

The frightened sheep huddled close to their youthful shepherd.

"It's all right," he spoke in soothing tones. "Never fear, my beauties, you are safe."

A few minutes later he led them up the gentle slope toward the pasture lands.

The sheep now spread out over the valley. The warm sun poured its rays down upon them.

"We must find a bit of shade soon," he said, as it grew hotter. "We will go down to that quiet pool, where you can drink; then I will let you rest in the shade."

For the remainder of the morning and through

the long afternoon young David watched over his sheep. He sang to them the songs he loved best. He spent another hour with his sling. When the sheep moved toward the upper end of the valley, he went ahead of them and rooted out some poisonous plants which grew there.

"I must prepare their table in the presence of enemies," he said. "No harm shall come to them from these poisonous weeds."

And now the shadows lengthened. It was time he led his flocks back home. One call brought them bounding toward him.

There was still one duty that he must perform as a good shepherd. Many times his sheep were stung between the ears by a sand fly that frequented the pastures. These wounds festered and grew very painful. It was the shepherd's task to discover this early. When his sheep arrived at the corral he set a staff across the entryway about a foot from the ground. Each sheep had to jump over the staff before he could enter.

David stood beside the door. As each sheep came by he parted the wool between its ears to see if it looked red and inflamed. Whenever he discovered a sheep with this swelling, he would take his horn of oil and anoint the spot. This brought almost instant relief.

At last the sheep were folded for the night.

King David awoke from his dream. He was not the shepherd lad in Bethlehem, but king of a

SONG OF THE SHEPHERD KING

strong nation. Then his thoughts took another turn.

"What a lesson we may learn from the life of the shepherd!" he mused. "There is a Great Shepherd, the All-Father, who cares for us just as I used to care for my sheep. He provides food and drink. He brings us cheer and comfort in the hours of danger. He anoints our heads with the oil of gladness."

David now penned that most beautiful Psalm that we all know so well.

The Lord is my shepherd; I shall not want. He maketh me to lie down in green pastures; he leadeth me beside the still waters. He restoreth my soul: he leadeth me in the paths of righteousness for his name's sake. Yea, though I walk through the valley of the shadow of death, I will fear no evil: for thou art with me; thy rod and thy staff they comfort me. Thou preparest a table before me in the presence of mine enemies: thou anointest my head with oil; my cup runneth over. Surely goodness and mercy shall follow me all the days of my life: and I will dwell in the house of the Lord for ever.

ABE LINCOLN'S HAPPY THANKSGIVING

"I'M full, mother," said little Abe, shoving back his three-legged stool from the table. "I just can't eat another bite."

"You fill up too soon," said his father, taking another drumstick of the wild turkey. "You must hurry up and be a man."

Mrs. Lincoln looked with loving eyes at her eight-year-old son. Already he was becoming long and lanky. He was much taller than the average child of his age.

"Now get some water and hang the kettle over the fire," said the mother. "Nancy and I will do the dishes and then I have another surprise for you."

"I wish Thanksgiving came every day," said Abe, looking wistfully at the well-browned turkey and jelly and rye bread plus all the other good things on the table.

"By the time you get the water you will be ready for the next treat," remarked his mother.

"What? Something more?" he asked.

The mother's head nodded.

"Hurray! Where is that pail?" With a rush the lad was on his way to the spring.

"Now put a log on the fire so it will burn quickly," she added, as he came puffing in with his pail of water.

ABE'S HAPPY THANKSGIVING

Then, going to the cupboard, she took out a plate with something brown and tempting on it. It was taffy made of maple syrup.

"Yum-yum," said Nancy, having a hard time getting her jaws open. "That's something more to be thankful for."

"Indeed, we have many things to thank God for this year," said the mother.

"So much more than the Pilgrims who first celebrated the day," continued Nancy.

"Oh, mother, do tell us about the first Thanksgiving," cried Abe.

"All right, children. While the water for the dishes is getting hot I will tell you what I know of it.

"Long years ago there were certain people in England who wanted to worship God as they chose. The king said they could not. So they left his country and went to Holland. That was not satisfactory, so they chartered a vessel and set sail for America.

"The Mayflower was not a large boat. More than a hundred persons were crowded onto her. You can imagine the hardships that these brave people endured.

"It was late in the fall when finally they sighted land. The captain had taken them far north of the place they expected to reach. So they decided to make their home along the shore of Cape Cod. Party after party went out to explore the country, but none found a satisfactory location.

WORLD OVER STORIES

"At last the mate of the vessel told of a landing he had made on a previous voyage.

" 'There is a good river for our vessel; there is a fine hill for your fort; and there are many trees with which to build.'

"The people decided to go there. It was in December that they finally landed at Plymouth.

"Now the work of housebuilding began. The men marked out a street and decided where each house and their fort should stand. Then they went to the forest and felled the trees. Before the winter became severe several houses were completed.

"What a hard winter was that first one!" said the mother.

"Almost as bad as ours last year in the half-face camp," piped up Abe.

"It was something like it, surely," his mother replied.

"Their rude huts were made of logs with moss and mud filled into the cracks. But the frost and snow did creep through. People fell sick. They had lived so long on the poor shipboard fare that they could not withstand the winter. One after another died. By spring only about half of their number was left.

"But they did not lose courage even then. The Indians showed them how to plant Indian corn and soon their fields were green with crops. The children spent their time in picking berries and gathering nuts. By fall they had enough food to last them through the winter.

ABE'S HAPPY THANKSGIVING

" 'Let us set aside a day of thanks to God for his bounties,' said their governor.

"A day was chosen. The mothers cooked the meat over the open fire and filled large baskets with corn bread. Dishes of jelly and fruits, and puddings such as they used to have in England were added.

"Their Indian friends came and enjoyed the feast with them. It was a notable occasion and lasted several days.

" 'This is a worthy custom,' said one of their leaders. 'I think it should be continued.'

" 'Let us plan a Thanksgiving day each year,' said the governor.

"Thus it came about that we have this day set aside," concluded Mrs. Lincoln.

"I am glad they had a first Thanksgiving," said Abe. "And now may I have some more taffy?"

STRONG IN VICTORY AND BRAVE IN DEFEAT

EVERY boy and girl in the Lincoln School was happy the day following their basketball victory over their rival, the Washington. As they passed one another in the halls such remarks as these might have been heard:

"We licked them, Jim."

"Sure we licked them. What else could you expect?"

"Yes, they are only a scrub bunch. We had to show them up."

These and a score of other slighting remarks came to the ears of Superintendent McClean. He thought it time to have a serious talk with his boys and girls concerning true sportsmanship.

"Students," he said at the assembly period, "we are all most happy over our victory of last night. After three years of defeat by the Washington, I, for one, am glad to have fortune come our way.

"But from the remarks I heard in the hall this morning I fear we are in serious danger of a worse defeat. I believe it is often a greater test of sportsmanship to win than to lose. When we lose, what do we do? We just grit our teeth and vow to do better next time. But when we win, what happens? We may get a false sense of

STRONG IN VICTORY AND DEFEAT

superiority and fail to show proper courtesy to a worthy opponent.

"To make my point clear I want to take you with me to a little cottage back in Michigan where my grandfather lives. He was a veteran in the Civil War and fought with Grant at the time of its close. I have heard him tell the story of Lee's surrender many times. These are about his words:

"We were sitting before the walls of Richmond. For four long years the boys of the North and the boys of the South had struggled back and forth across the border, leaving suffering and destruction in their wake. But now Sherman had made his march to the sea, and our general, Grant, was closing in about General Lee.

"We did not know exactly how large an army he had. We could only estimate that he was fighting our quarter of a million with some thirty thousand men. Later we found out the sad condition of his army. His men were dying each day from disease and starvation. They were so hard pressed for food that they ate the corn intended for the horses. Munitions were low and medicine for the sick was gone.

"Lee knew that there was but one possibility for him. If he could join the army of Johnston in the west, he would escape the clutches of Grant. But our general was not to be tricked in that way. By forced marches we cut off Lee's line of retreat. We knew, as well as did Lee, that further struggle was useless.

WORLD OVER STORIES

"We fellows now began planning the terms of surrender that we would make. About the campfires at night you might hear such remarks as these:

" 'Just a few days more, boys, and we'll make the rebels pay.'

" 'Indeed they will pay,' another would speak up. 'They marched through my country and burned everything. Let them give me back my stock.'

" 'Let them pay the whole cost of the war,' a third would chime in. 'They brought it on.'

" 'We'll hang Jeff Davis on a sour-apple tree,' another began to sing and the group joined heartily in the song. This was the thought of the men in the ranks.

"One morning we saw our general, Grant, and some of his staff mount their horses and ride quickly away. We learned later that he and General Lee had met at Appomattox village for a conference. They were talking over the terms of surrender. And what do you think General Grant proposed? Did he ask the sort of thing we men had been asking? No, indeed. He did not take an unfair advantage of a defeated foe. He was as strong in victory as was Lee in defeat. He was a true gentleman and set a proper example of courtesy.

"What were the terms of surrender? Grant only asked that the Southern soldiers lay down their arms. No officer would be required to give up his sword or side-arms—a concession seldom

STRONG IN VICTORY AND DEFEAT

made to a defeated army. As to the horses—well, our general said with a smile, the boys in gray might need them for the fall plowing. Then these two great generals shook hands and returned to the ranks. Now what do you think of that?

"When we soldiers heard of the surrender we wanted to celebrate. Surely, after four years of fighting we were justified in having a bit of noise and celebration. But, no, sir! We had hardly shot off a single cannon when General Grant put a stop to it.

"'Those brave men feel their defeat bad enough now, boys,' he said. 'We shouldn't make it harder for them.'

"Neither would he ride into Richmond lest it be considered somewhat like a triumphal entry.

"That was the gentlemanly spirit of our general. He had a proper respect for his opponent and would do nothing that would needlessly offend. That was what I call true sportsmanship."

"And that," concluded the superintendent, "is the spirit I hope we may cultivate. It is often as great a test of manhood and womanhood to be strong in victory as to be brave in defeat."

A HEROIC FRIENDSHIP

THE two boys, Damon and Pythias, rushed out of their school in the ancient city of Syracuse and started toward the blue Adriatic for a swim.

"I'll beat you to the float," shouted Damon as they came to the pebbly beach. In a short time both boys were plunging through the balmy waters in their efforts to reach the distant buoy.

When finally they reached their goal, they hung to the dancing buoy and looked back at the picture behind them. The rich blue waters of the Adriatic formed the foreground of that picture. Beyond that lay the city of red-tiled roofs and yellow walls. The wharves of the shore were crowded with trading vessels of every description, some of them bearing strange designs on their sails, waiting for their cargo for some far-away, mysterious port. In the distant background lay the purpling hills touched with the crimson light of the waning sun.

"Damon, do you realize that we must soon take military training?" said Pythias after a short silence. "I hope we can be together in the same company."

"So do I," answered Damon, placing his hand on the shoulder of his bosom pal. "I suppose you will become a soldier when you are through."

A HEROIC FRIENDSHIP

"Indeed I will," replied Pythias, grandly. "Father will help me become an officer in the army, and some of these days I will be a great general. You can ride with me in my chariot, Damon, when I make my triumphal entry into the city." Both boys laughed heartily over this bit of boasting.

"I'm just going to be a farmer," said Damon, quietly. "I will act as overseer for father on his plantations. I like to be at the country villa with the fountains and gardens of fragrant flowers. You can come to visit me there after you finish your triumphal entry."

Thus the two boys planned their future, little realizing that the dreams of youth were to be realized later. But their natural preferences soon led them into the activities they enjoyed best. Pythias, strong of limb and natural-born adventurer, turned to the excitement of the camp and the hardships of distant campaigns. His manly courage and wisdom made him beloved of the soldiers, who would follow him into any danger. In time he became the great general of whom he had dreamed and led the armies to victory.

Damon took over the many estates of his father and managed them so well that he became a wealthy and noted man. In time he was elected to the Senate of Syracuse and was looked upon as a statesman of prudence.

Even though separated, the loyalty and friendship of these two men never waned. If anything, it increased with the years. The words "Damon and Pythias" became the common expression for a true and lasting friendship.

Years passed by. Pythias had just returned victor from a hard-fought campaign. As was his custom he went to the home of Damon for rest. As the two men walked among the sparkling fountains they talked of their city and the dangers that seemed so near. Dionysius, a man of low birth and of little honor, was endeavoring to make himself tyrant of the city.

"Do you know, Pythias, I fear Dionysius will try to have himself proclaimed king in the near future."

"Can it be possible?" said the general, with troubled brow. "A black curse will fall on our fair city if he gains control."

Their worst fears were soon to be realized. Dionysius, the man of whom they spoke, was at that very time bribing certain senators to help him with his base plans. He made great promises of riches and honor to those who would help him to power, promises which he had no intention of keeping.

Within a week from the time of Damon's prophecy one of the senators rose in the senate chamber and moved that the city be given over to Dionysius. Most of the senators were absent and those present were the followers of this politician. The motion was carried. Dionysius was made king. He gathered his soldiers about him and awaited developments.

A HEROIC FRIENDSHIP

When the news of this move came to Damon on his plantation, he mounted horse and rushed away to the city. He hoped to show the members of the Senate the danger that would follow such a move. As he set foot in the senate halls he was arrested as an enemy of the New Republic and was sentenced to die at sunset. Soldiers led him away to the prison to await the hour of execution.

Suddenly he was startled from his dark musings by the presence of his friend, Pythias. The latter had heard of the king's action and of Damon's arrest. Knowing that Damon would want to return home to settle his affairs, he had hastened to the newly elected monarch and asked that he, Pythias, might take Damon's place in the prison.

At first the king refused permission. Then an ugly gleam overspread his countenance. He hated both of these men and suddenly realized that here was a chance to be rid of them both.

"Go," he said, loudly, "take your place in the prison. But remember that if Damon is not back with the setting of the sun, you shall die in his place." Then the king secretly commanded his soldiers to follow Damon when he was released and to kill him on the road.

Now Pythias became the prisoner and his friend sped away to his home. Much needed to be done and the time was short. Rapidly he worked setting his accounts to rights and giving instructions to his foremen what to do. Then as

WORLD OVER STORIES

the hour of sunset approached he told his beautiful wife of the fate that awaited him.

"Oh, Damon, you cannot go, you shall not go!" cried the lady.

"I have promised," he answered, quietly.

Back in the city the soldiers were gathering in the public square for an execution. The evening shadows were lengthening. Pythias in his prison cell could see that the orb of the sun was approaching the rim of the western hills. If Damon did not return before it sank from sight, he must die. Soldiers came and led him to the public square. There amid the multitude were the executioner and the block.

"He will come," said the man as the sun sank along the horizon.

The king taunted him.

"Where is this wonderful friend for whom you risked your life? See, he has deserted you."

But Pythias answered with a smile, "He will come."

The sun was getting lower and lower. Now but half of it showed over the mountaintop, now but a fourth.

"Still he will come," said Pythias, confidently.

The crowd stood tense and silent. The executioner tested the edge of his ax. In a minute more Pythias must die.

Then suddenly a stir occurred on the outer edge of the crowd.

"Damon, Damon; he is here!" rose the voice of the multitude.

A HEROIC FRIENDSHIP

A young man, blood-bespattered and spent, stumbled forward through the throng. Quickly he made his way to the platform and mounted it. The two lifelong friends grasped hands in a new bond of friendship.

This loyalty on the part of the men touched the better nature of the king.

"Set the prisoners free," he commanded. "Such friendship shall not perish."

And thus it is that the names of Damon and Pythias remain even to this day as the expression of a true and lasting friendship.

THE MAID OF BETHLEHEM

"OH, mother, it's such fun," cried little Ruth, rushing up the stone steps of her home in ancient Bethlehem. "There are lots and lots of people from strange countries pouring into town."

Indeed, the hill city of Bethlehem *was* becoming crowded with Jews. A law had gone out from Cæsar that all persons of the world should be taxed and that they must enroll in their home city. Jews were therefore coming from Rome and distant Babylon. Their brightly colored garments were dust-covered and travel-stained.

"I saw a man with a turban on his head. His camel was snow-white. I think he must have come from India. He talked so strangely," continued the little girl, seating herself on the stone bench within the house.

"Are they finding places to stay?" asked the mother, as she prepared the supper. "It is going to be a hard job to find lodging for so many, and the nights are too cold to sleep comfortably outside."

"The tavern is full now," said Ruth, who had spent much of the day mingling with the throng. "Donkeys and camels and horses are all mixed up in the courtyard."

The supper hour was wholly consumed by Ruth in telling of her adventures of the day.

THE MAID OF BETHLEHEM

"I only wish David and father were here to enjoy it with us," concluded Ruth, thinking of her brother and father now out on the hillside with the sheep.

"We must not neglect the sheep," said the mother. "They have to be fed regardless of the decrees of Cæsar."

After the evening meal mother and daughter climbed to the top of their flat-roofed dwelling and looked down upon the scene below. Their home was on the road that led from Jerusalem to Bethlehem and they had a splendid view of the fields of "Boaz" as well as of the city itself.

"Here come another man and woman," said Ruth, a little later. "How tired they look! The man walks as though he had made a long journey and the woman leans heavily on the donkey."

"I believe it is Joseph of Nazareth," whispered the mother, as they came by the dwelling. "He is related to the tavern-keeper and should find lodging there."

The travelers passed on toward the tavern.

Early the next morning Jacob, Ruth's father, burst into the house.

"What has happened? Is David hurt?" cried the mother in dismay.

"No, mother, David is all right; but I have a strange story to tell you," said Jacob.

The father then proceeded to tell of the unusual happenings of the previous night.

"It was my turn to take care of the sheep during the first watch," said Jacob. "The other men had gone to sleep on their sheepskin robes and I had fixed the fire.

"I was drowsing myself, I guess, when suddenly I heard the sheep become restless. As I looked up it seemed that the hillside was lighted more than usual. The light grew brighter and brighter. Then a star of unusual brightness seemed to be right above me. I woke the other men and we watched the light.

"Suddenly out of the brightness came an angel, dressed in flowing garments of pure white. You may be sure we were frightened. We fell on our faces to the ground.

"The angel said, 'Fear not; for, behold, I bring you tidings of great joy, which shall be to all people. For unto you is born this day in the city of David a Saviour, which is Christ the Lord. And this shall be a sign unto you; Ye shall find the babe wrapped in swaddling clothes, lying in a manger.'

"We had looked up while the angel was saying these words. Imagine our amazement to see a host of angels with their leader, now speaking to us, and saying, 'Glory to God in the highest, and on earth peace, good will toward men.'

"Then this heavenly group vanished from our sight and only our fire of sticks lighted the darkness.

"'What shall we do?' asked Moses, our kinsman.

"'I think we should go at once to the city and see what has happened,' counseled James.

THE MAID OF BETHLEHEM

" 'That is right,' I answered. 'David, you care for the sheep while we are gone.'

"Thereupon we hastened away and were soon at the sheep cave behind the tavern. Surely enough, there were Joseph and Mary and the Babe in the manger as the angel had said.

" 'Blessings on you, O blessed of God,' said the aged Moses as we came to them. Then we told of the strange message of the angels."

"What can it mean?" asked Naomi, when Jacob had concluded.

"I know not unless the prophecy of Isaiah is now to be fulfilled," said the father.

"Oh, mamma," cried Ruth, "may I take some lamb's broth to Mary? She looked so worn and tired last night as she passed."

"Thoughtful child," said Naomi, looking at her little daughter with loving eyes. "While we talk of what it may mean you remember that someone is in need of help. Indeed you may take the broth. I will fix it at once."

Within a few minutes Ruth was hastening along the crooked street toward the sheepfold behind the tavern. She hesitated as she entered.

"What is it, my child?" called Mary, seeing the little girl standing in the entry way.

"My father just told us of the Wonder-Child who has been born," answered Ruth, "and I thought you might like some lamb's broth. You looked so weary as you passed our home last night."

"May the blessings of our fathers be upon you

for your kindly deed," said Joseph, who stood beside Mary.

Then, taking her by the hand, he led her toward the manger where the Christ-child lay.

"If the message of the angels comes true," he continued, "this little one may, some day, be the Great Helper of our nation and of mankind. Perhaps you can be a partner with him in doing kindly deeds."

Thus Ruth had her first glimpse of **Jesus, the Christ**.

THE MAN WHO BETRAYED HIS COUNTRY

COWARD. Traitor. How sadly we remember the dark blot that hangs over his name! Benedict Arnold, general in the Revolutionary War, was a man seemingly honest and sincere. He gained the confidence of George Washington and was given a position of high honor. Then suddenly he turned about-face, proved false to his trust, and tried to sell his country to the enemy for a few pieces of silver. We study this man's life only that we may avoid such unfaithfulness in any form.

The early career of Arnold shows him to have been a bold, dashing, fearless leader. He left home at the age of fifteen to join the American forces in the French and Indian War. Next we hear of him with Ethan Allen and the Green Mountain boys in the attack on Fort Ticonderoga. His bravery here quickly gained him a high command in the army. When in 1775 he led the march on Quebec he showed such bravery and good sense that Washington asked that he be made major-general.

But at this point the darker side of his character began to show. Seemingly he did not love his country. His chief concern was for himself. He wanted to be talked of as a great general and to be praised and applauded. When he saw other men made major-generals while he still held his old rank he became very angry. He decided to sell his country to the British.

We can understand just what he did if we remember how hard a struggle our country was having at that time. For five painful years our soldiers had been fighting against the greatest nation of the world. The British had plenty of men, of guns, and of ammunition. Our soldiers were just common farmers and business men, untrained as warriors, and often without enough ammunition. When they fell sick there was scarcely any medicine to be had. They were entirely without pay. The winter at Valley Forge, where the mark of blood showed in their footprints, tells vividly of the hardships and suffering they bore. Yet these patriots were loyal to their leader and their country.

At such a time Arnold planned his revenge. He went to Washington and asked to be made commander of West Point, one of the most important points of the colonists. Whichever army held this fort could control the surrounding country. Washington had such faith in him that he made the man his general there.

As soon as Arnold was located at this fort he began plotting with the British. He drew maps of the fort and surrounding country, and showed the best means of attack and the chief weaknesses of his position. Then he sent for Major André, of the British Army, and turned these maps over to him. Luckily André was captured before he

MAN WHO BETRAYED COUNTRY

got back to the British lines, so the enemy never had a chance to make use of the maps.

Arnold was having a banquet with some of his officers when he first learned of André's capture. No one of the group ever dreamed that he had a hand in this affair. He asked to be excused from the table, slipped into the back yard, flung himself onto his horse, and escaped to the British lines.

What was he to receive—this traitor to his country—for his black deed? The British promised him wealth and a high position in their army.

But Arnold was soon to suffer for his bargain. He expected to go to London after the war and be received as a great man. He found when he got there that people had little respect for a man who sold his country. The Tories, the more cultured class, refused to admit him into their group. He was soon an outcast in society. The money he was to receive from the government was not enough to keep him, and the man was reduced to poverty.

As he grew older he withdrew from the company of others. The shame he felt for having sold his post of duty caused him to stay alone in his old home, served by one aged servant. When he was about to die he called for the uniform he had worn as an officer in the ranks under Washington. Tearfully he put it on, saying to his servant, "Would God I had never worn any other." Thus died the man who proved false to his country.

THE HERO OF THE FEVER ZONE

"ARE we surely going, father? Are we really going to sail through the Panama Canal?"

"Yes, my son," answered Mr. Willoughby. "Mother and I think such a trip would be as profitable for us all as any we could make."

"Whoopee!" shouted Dick. "It certainly suits me."

"But, my lad," said the father, "you will not be ready to go until you have studied all about this canal, its past history and its present method of operation. We must be able to appreciate what we see. Suppose you look up the history part first."

For a couple of days nothing more was said of Panama. Then the father decided to see what his son had discovered.

"Who was President of the United States, Dick, when the Panama Canal was taken over by this country?"

"President Roosevelt, father," came back the quick reply. "We bought out the rights of the French on May 4, 1904."

"Fine, fine," was the father's comment. "Now tell me something about this French company."

"I read in one of the books about the man who projected the idea, a Mr. De Lesseps. He was

THE HERO OF THE FEVER ZONE

the man who built the Suez Canal and because of his success there the French people had much confidence in him. They voted him three hundred million dollars to build the canal over here. In 1879 the French Panama Canal Company was formed and the work was begun."

"I see you have been making good use of your history books," said Mr. Willoughby, with a smile. "Now tell me why it was that they did not succeed."

"There were several reasons," continued Dick. "One was the indifference and even dishonesty of those who were working with De Lesseps. According to what I read, a considerable amount of the money voted went into the pockets of these men.

"The chief enemy, however, was fever and disease. Malaria, yellow fever, and plague followed them everywhere. They built large hospitals and did all they could to stop it, but their men died like flies. After a few years of valueless work they abandoned the dredges and cars in the ditches. They quit."

"That was a good report, son," said the father. "Now I want to tell you of an unknown hero of these days who played a large part in making the canal a success. To tell of him I will begin where you left off.

"President Roosevelt chose the most skilled men he could find to build this canal. These men went to Panama and studied the situation carefully. They realized that they must face the same enemy that De Lesseps faced, and that unless they could overcome this fever they would fail just as he had failed.

"Immediately questions came up as to the nature of malaria, yellow fever, and plague. What caused them? How were they carried? Under what conditions were they most deadly? To answer these questions they turned back to two pioneers in this field, Doctors Lazear and Carrol, by name, who had tried to drive yellow fever out of Cuba. It was four years previous that an epidemic of yellow fever had broken out in Havana, Cuba. The American government sent a Health Commission to the island to study the cause of the disease and its possible prevention and cure. In this commission were two doctors, our hero and Doctor Carrol. After looking over the situation thoroughly they decided to test out the ideas as to the cause of yellow fever. The Cubans claimed that if one touched the clothes or bedding of a sick person, he in turn would catch the disease. They said that it had been brought to the island by passengers from a trading vessel.

"The Health Commission decided to test this theory first. They built a small cabin in one of the hottest quarters of the city of Havana. The windows and doors were carefully screened. They put strong locks on the doors so that no one could enter or leave without their consent. Three men were placed in this cabin. For twenty days these men stayed in this stifling house with

THE HERO OF THE FEVER ZONE

the temperature averaging from ninety to a hundred. Each day the doctors brought clothes, bedding, and dishes used by persons who were sick with the fever. The men wore the clothes. They slept on the blankets. In every possible way they exposed themselves to the disease, in order to see if it could be caught by handling such articles. After twenty days they came out as well as when they went in. This seemed like conclusive proof that the fever was not spread by contact with the clothes or bedding of people sick with the fever.

Another theory as to the spread of malaria had to do with the mosquito. Several of the doctors thought that the mosquito was the common carrier of the disease. If the mosquito stung a sick person and later stung one who was well, the latter person was likely to come down with the disease. There was only one way to be sure and that was to try it out.

"But such an experiment was dangerous. To be stung by a mosquito might mean death in a few days. Despite this fact the two doctors, Lazear and Carrol, offered themselves for the test. They were taken to the hospital. They allowed a mosquito to sting a patient who was very low with the disease and later to sting them. In a few days both men were delirious as a result of the infection. Doctor Lazear never recovered. He was truly a martyr for the cause of humanity. This hero soul made himself a sacrifice so that others would not have to suffer and die. These

WORLD OVER STORIES

two doctors had proven that the mosquito was the carrier of this dreaded fever germ.

"The knowledge gained in 1900 by these brave and consecrated men was now to be put to use at the Canal Zone. President Roosevelt gave Doctor Gorgas complete control of the health measures. His task was to destroy the mosquito by stamping out its breeding places. Where do mosquitoes breed, son?"

"In any stagnant water," answered Dick.

"That is right. Therefore Doctor Gorgas must find all the places where water stood. He had whole brigades of men go about covering the swamps with oil. The little film that covers the water does not allow the baby mosquito to come to the surface for air, and he suffocates. Other men roamed the streets killing all adult mosquitoes. Houses were screened. Running water was turned into the filth-ridden streets and houses. If any person became ill, he was at once rushed to the quarantine station. Such rigid measures have made the Canal Zone as safe from the fever as our own city is.

"That is the story of these early days in the Canal Zone, Dick. Our United States is proud to have completed the task. But we should not forget those unsung heroes, whose sacrifice of themselves made this success possible."

KINDNESS REWARDED

ON the outskirts of an African village lived Simpu and his wife. This aged couple were among the most destitute of the village. Their hut was always in bad repair and their fields never would yield a good crop. Often Simpu and his wife went to bed hungry.

"Why do we always have such bad luck?" complained the woman.

"Perhaps we have offended the gods," replied her patient husband. "But let us hope. Some day our luck will change."

Even the following year when hail destroyed his crops and he was laid up with rheumatism, the man would say: "Let us still hope. Our luck will change."

Then there came a year of plenty for Simpu. His millet fields bore an abundant crop and his berries were more plentiful than any of his neighbors.

"Why do you let the birds eat your berries?" said his neighbors scornfully. "Why don't you drive them away as we do?"

"Let them eat," said the kind-hearted man. "I know what it means to go to bed hungry. Why should I drive them away? There is enough for all of us."

So it happened that the birds of the forest often came to his fields. Simpu loved these feathered

WORLD OVER STORIES

friends and would talk to them as he worked among his vines.

One hot day in summer Simpu lay down under a tree at noontime and fell asleep. Some of his bird friends came to his field just at this hour. They saw him lying there in the shade and thought he was dead. Quickly they flew back to the King of Birds in the forest.

"Our friend and helper, Simpu, is dead," they announced to the King.

"What? Our benefactor dead? Come, my friends, we must give him a proper burial."

With that he gathered a squadron of his birds about him and flew toward the field of Simpu. They saw him lying in the shade on an old blanket.

"Seize hold of the blanket," commanded their leader, "and follow me."

What was Simpu's surprise a few minutes later to find himself being carried on his blanket far above the tops of the trees. It seemed to him that they were traveling in a northerly direction. For fear lest they should let go he said not a word.

On and on they flew until they came at last to the far-away mountains. Their leader took a straight course toward a lonely valley among the peaks. As they came still nearer, a cave appeared in the side of the cliff. The birds took him within this cave.

"Cover him with the blanket and let us be gone," said the King. There was a flutter of wings and Simpu was now alone.

KINDNESS REWARDED

"What shall I do; what shall I do?" said Simpu, looking around in dismay. "I am far from home and without food. It will be days before I can get back to my mud hut in the village."

The old man rose stiffly and shuffled toward the mouth of the cave. As he did so his foot kicked some of the pebbles on the ground. They sparkled and gleamed in the sunlight. Simpu was on his knees in a minute examining them.

"Gold," he shouted in glee. "Gold, gold, and lots of it. I knew our luck would change!"

Spreading his blanket on the ground, he gathered as many nuggets of the precious metal as he could conveniently carry. Then he set off for home.

Three days later, as the evening shadows darkened, a weary but happy man crept into the village and made his way to his mud hut. His wife was overjoyed to see him again, for she thought him dead. But far greater was her surprise when he opened his blanket and showed her the sparkling gold within.

"Where did you get it, my husband?" cried the excited woman.

Simpu told her of his strange adventure.

"Come, we must bury our treasure at once, lest someone steal it from us."

From that time forth Simpu and his wife lived more comfortably. They repaired their house and made additions to it. They had all the food that was necessary. And from the white traders

WORLD OVER STORIES

they purchased many things that made life more enjoyable. Finally they decided to give a banquet for all their friends in the village to celebrate their good fortune.

"Where did you get the money to buy such a feast?" asked the guests as they ate of the fine food. Simpu told them frankly of his unusual experience with the birds and how he had discovered gold in the mountains.

One of his guests that day was Sinabe, the most selfish and meanest man in all the village. Sinabe waited when all the other guests had gone to ask Simpu more about his adventure.

"May I work in your field to-morrow?" asked Sinabe, with a crafty look. He was thinking of all the gold he might carry away.

"Surely, my friend," replied the kindly Simpu. "I hope that the birds may find you also and carry you to the cave in the mountains."

The next morning bright and early Sinabe was in the field of his friend. He worked with a will and was truly tired when he lay down at noontime on his blanket. If one had looked carefully he might have seen several sacks tucked away under him.

Promptly at noon the birds came again for their usual meal. Seeing a man lying under the tree as if dead they hastened, a second time, to their King.

"Another man is lying dead in the field of Simpu," they said. "It is Sinabe, who has tried many times to kill us."

KINDNESS REWARDED

"What? Sinabe dead?" replied the King. "Come, my friends, we must also give him a decent burial."

Again the squadron of birds flew to the field of Simpu. They plucked the blanket of the sleeping man in their beaks and rose above the forest. But now their leader turned southward. Hour after hour they sped along, over mountain and valley. When the setting sun touched the clouds with crimson still they were flying southward. When the night had completely fallen, they yet traveled on.

Some time during the night Sinabe felt himself being lowered to the earth. He could not see where he was but the feel of the ground proved that it was mountainous country. He eagerly awaited the dawn.

"Where is the cave?" muttered the man as the first light streaked the east. "And where is the gold?"

All that day the greedy peasant hunted among the peaks, and all the next day. He found nothing that faintly resembled gold.

A full week afterward a haggard and weary man straggled back into the mud huts of his tribe carrying several empty sacks. He had nothing to show for his much labor.

(Based on an African legend.)

FRIEND OF THE FRIENDLESS [1]

IN the Temple prison at Jerusalem three men were awaiting their time of execution.

Barabbas, bold and reckless chieftain, had led a revolt against the Roman masters. He with his two companions, Simon and Melchior, was now awaiting his fate.

"What time is it?" called he through his cell door.

"It must be nearing ten o'clock," answered Melchior from the adjoining cell.

"We will not have long to wait," said Simon. "The soldiers will soon lead us forth."

"There is yet one chance," said Barabbas. "It is the custom to release one prisoner at Passover time. Possibly one of you will be freed. They would scarcely free a murderer and rebel."

"Your hopes are groundless," answered Simon. "The Romans know how to take care of those who revolt."

As they spoke there came the distant tramp, tramp, tramp of soldier feet in the dim passageway. Nearer and nearer they came. Barabbas expected surely that they would stop at his cell. But instead, they went on to that of Melchior. A moment later he saw his companion disappear between four soldiers.

---

[1] This is an imaginative story based on the biblical account and an ancient Jewish tradition.

FRIEND OF THE FRIENDLESS

"Melchior is gone," called Simon. "I wonder whether it is to freedom or to death?"

"Who can tell?" said the young man, and lapsed into silence. In his mind's eye he followed Melchior out of the prison into the bright sunlight of day. He saw himself as a child again, roaming through the market place, or going to the synagogue school. He saw his humble home and his invalid mother sitting by the window as usual.

His revery was broken by the approach of the soldiers again. This time they stopped at the cell of Simon.

"Being the leader of this revolt they are saving me for the last," he said with a harsh laugh. "I will show them that I can die like a man."

Now came the soldiers a third time. The door creaked on its hinges as the four men entered the room. Seizing him they led him along the dark corridor, up the winding stairs, and to the entry way above. Here the leader paused and said: "Barabbas, you are free. Jesus Christ is dying in your place."

The young man stood blinking in the sunlight. His eyes were slow to adjust to the dazzling brightness of the noonday and his mind was equally slow in grasping what they said. Again the leader spoke: "Go where you will, Barabbas. You are free. Jesus Christ is dying in your stead."

Barabbas left the prison as in a dream. Strange, passing strange, that he should be liberated! More than strange that another was dying in his place. Jesus Christ. Jesus—ah yes, now he remembered where he had seen the man. It was more than two years before on a hillside near the Sea of Galilee. He had gone with the multitude to listen to this wonderful Man. All afternoon he had stayed, hearing those words of wisdom. Even yet he could remember that gentle voice saying: "Be kind; be merciful; be pure. Let your light so shine before men that they may see your good works and glorify your Father who is in heaven."

"He was a good man," mused Barabbas. "That day he did many kindly deeds. He healed the sick and brought sight to the blind. What has he done to warrant death?"

Little realizing where he went, Barabbas found himself on the way home. It had been many a day since he had gone through the door of their humble dwelling. But now he was free and could go where he chose. He would go to his mother to tell her of his good fortune. She would be sitting in her chair by the window as usual, he thought.

Imagine his surprise, when he entered the house, to find his mother walking around.

"My son, my son," cried the mother, joyfully, rushing forward and throwing her arms around his neck.

"But, mother," said Barabbas, in bewilderment, "how is it you walk?"

"A miracle has been performed," said the

FRIEND OF THE FRIENDLESS

mother. "It was last Sunday when we heard that Jesus approached the city. Kind friends carried me far along the road from the north so that we might avoid the throng. As he passed I cried, 'Master, have mercy!' He paused and looked at me, saying, 'Be of good cheer. Thy faith hath made thee whole.' From that moment strength returned to my limbs and I could walk."

Then the mother's face clouded and tears came into her eyes.

"But oh, Barabbas, to-day they have led him away to Calvary to crucify him. The chief priests hated him because he did deeds of kindness on the Sabbath day. They had a false trial and have condemned him to death."

Suddenly a light broke in on Barabbas. Now he understood what the leader had meant when he said, "Jesus Christ is dying in your stead." There had been a trial. Probably someone, perhaps Pilate, had asked who should be released at their feast time. He could almost hear their cries, "Barabbas, Barabbas! Release unto us Barabbas, and crucify this man!" By Christ's death he now had his freedom.

"Mother, I must be gone," he said. "I will go to Calvary. Perhaps there is still something that I can do for him who has done so much for you and me."

Leaving the house, Barabbas rushed headlong through the deserted streets and out of the city gate. Breathless he came to Calvary's hill. He elbowed his way through the throng and finally stood among the inner circle. There, upon the central cross, hung the Christ.

"O Master, it was you who befriended me when friendless. Is there aught I can do for you?" he cried. Eagerly he looked upon the face of the Christ.

Did those lips move? Barabbas could not be sure. It almost seemed that he could hear a voice saying: "Be kind; be merciful; be pure. Let your light so shine before men that they may see your good works and glorify your Father who is in heaven."

Hours later Barabbas found himself wandering the hillside. "That was his command," he mused. "That was what he wanted me to do. I, in turn, must be friend of the friendless."

THE BELOVED BISHOP

THE little French city of Digne, nestling among the foothills of the Alps, had one citizen of whom it could justly be proud. This was the venerable bishop, Monsieur Myriel. This aged man, beloved by all the people, had given his entire life to helping the poor. There was scarcely a peasant's hut in all the foothills where he had not gone on his errands of mercy. Even the robbers had respect for him, for had he not spent a fortnight in their fastnesses trying to win them over to a better life?

The home of the bishop, on this bleak October night in 1815, was thrown into confusion when Madame Magloire, the bishop's sister and housekeeper, told of a strange tramp, an ill-looking prowler, who had entered the city late that evening. Folks said that he was a prisoner who had been a galley slave for many years, and that it would be dangerous to meet him unprotected after dark.

Hardly had the woman stopped speaking when the outer door of the house was thrown open and a strange man entered. As he came into the light he was blinded for a moment, allowing those within a chance to note his appearance. His knapsack was on his shoulder and he carried a large club in his hand. A rough, bold expression was on his face; in the flickering glow of the firelight it looked murderous.

"I am Jean Valjean," he said, harshly. "I am a galley slave and have spent nineteen years in imprisonment. I want something to eat and I want it quick." The glowering eyes of the man stared hard at each inmate of the room.

"Come right in, my friend," said the kindly bishop with easy grace. "You are welcome, thrice welcome. We have been waiting for you. Madame Magloire, did you lay the extra knife and fork?"

As Jean Valjean heard these words he stood as one in a daze.

"Wait, wait a minute," he cried out, as though they had not understood him. "That will not do. I did not want to eat with you. I only wanted food. Did you not hear me say that I was a bad man? See; here is my yellow card. It says that I have been on the galley ship nineteen years; five years for robbery and fourteen years for trying to escape. But I have money. I can pay."

"Sit down and warm yourself, friend," said the bishop. "This is God's house, not mine. You are always welcome. We will eat together in a few minutes. In the meantime I will have your cot made ready."

Suddenly it dawned upon Jean Valjean that a human being was showing him kindness. In all the years of his life, since he stood at his mother's knee, no one had ever before been kind to him or called him a friend. The harsh light

THE BELOVED BISHOP

faded out of his eyes and in its place came first a look of wonder, then doubt, and finally joy.

How strange it seemed! Quickly his mind reverted to those years on board the galley ship, those long years of human torture, the cannon ball tied to the foot, the plank to sleep on, the red jacket, floggings, heat, cold, the dungeon. And never a single word of kindness.

He seemed to be awaking from a dream as he heard the bishop say: "You did not need to tell me who you were. I knew before you spoke. You are my brother. All that we have is yours. You are suffering; you are hungry and thirsty; your wants shall be supplied." With that the bishop made ready for the evening meal.

That supper was one ever to be remembered by Jean Valjean. Here was white linen spread in his honor. The best silverware was brought out. Even the silver candlesticks were taken from the cabinet that their warm, mellow glow might make the occasion more comfortable and homelike.

Jean Valjean ate ravenously of the food. For days his starved body had been without proper nourishment and now he could scarce get his fill.

After the meal the bishop bade his sister good night. Taking one of the candlesticks from the table he gave the other to his guest and led the way toward the bed chamber. It so happened that the bishop's room was next to that of the ex-convict. When Jean noticed this he turned upon the old man and said:

WORLD OVER STORIES

"What? Would you really lodge me as close to you as that? How do you know that I will not kill you during the night?"

"That is between you and God," came the quiet answer of the bishop. Then with outstretched arm the bishop spoke a word of blessing on his guest and departed from the room without so much as turning his head.

Jean Valjean slept poorly that night. For hours he pitched and tossed. As the clock in the cathedral tower struck two he became fully awake. Strange, murderous thoughts raced through his feverish mind. Now was his chance for revenge. Society had been unjust to him, now he would get even with society.

He slipped quickly from his bed and seized the heavy bar from his knapsack. Then with the stealth of a cat he approached the door of the sleeping bishop.

The door of the bishop's room was open. He was sleeping peacefully, wrapped in a long garment of brown wool. His face was lighted up by the moonlight that flooded through the window and disclosed an expression of peacefulness and hope. There was something almost akin to divinity in the placid countenance of the sleeper.

As Valjean looked his conscience smote him. A kind of terror gripped his very soul. His powerful limbs trembled and his breath came in quick gasps.

Then the sight of the silvern candlesticks

THE BELOVED BISHOP

brought him back to reality. Snatching them up he leaped through the open window to the garden, bounded over the stone wall like a tiger, and was lost in the semigloom.

However, his freedom was short-lived. As the bishop and his sister were leaving the breakfast table the following morning there came a knock at the door. Three soldiers and a corporal thrust a struggling man through the door and confronted the bishop.

"Ah, so you have returned, my brother," said the bishop with warmest welcome. "I am most glad. You took the candlesticks as I directed, but left the silverware. They also were yours. Take them. They will bring you two hundred francs."

Both the soldiers and Jean Valjean stood aghast at these words.

"Monsigneur," said the leader, "what this man told us is then true? You did give him the candlesticks?"

"In very truth, my friends, and the silverware as well."

"In that case we can let him go," said the corporal.

The soldiers loosened their hold on the man, who tottered back and would have fallen.

"Is it true that I am not to go back to the galleys?" he asked in surprise.

The bishop now placed his hands on the shoulders of the trembling ex-convict and said to him in a low voice:

WORLD OVER STORIES

"Jean Valjean, my brother, you no longer belong to evil but to good. I have bought your soul from you. I withdraw it from black thoughts and the spirit of wrong and give it back to God."

Valjean stood before the house of the bishop in the warm October sunlight. In his hands were the silverware and candlesticks, gifts of the bishop. But a greater gift had been given—the gift of sympathy and human kindness. From that day forth his life was lived in making others more happy.

(Adapted from *Les Misérables*,
by Victor Hugo.)

THOSE WHO LOVE THE FLAG

IT was Armistice Day. Old Mr. Tucker, veteran of the Civil War, hobbled painfully down town to watch the parade go by. He had hardly gained his vantage point at the post office when the music of the band told of its near approach. Beside him stood two neighbor boys, Robert and Phil, who were craning their necks to see the procession.

"Remove your hats, boys, for the flag is passing by," spoke Mr. Tucker as the procession came abreast of them.

"It's only the flag," said Phil, thoughtlessly.

"Only the flag?" said the old veteran with a quick intake of breath. Then in a kindly voice he added, "Yes, laddie, it is only the flag, but some are willing to die for it."

That was all that was said at the time, and Phil might have forgotten the incident if he had not received a package the next day.

"Here is a present someone left for you," said his mother at the dinner table. "What do you suppose it is?"

"It's a book," replied Phil, hastily tearing off the wrapper. "It says, 'From Daddy Tucker to my young friend Philip. May he read this book and think long of its message.'"

Philip sat down and read the following story:

It was a tense moment in the trial of Philip Nolan that September day in 1807. Old Colonel

WORLD OVER STORIES

Morgan, of Revolutionary fame, was acting as judge, and about him, as jurors, were a score of men who had served with Washington at Trenton and Valley Forge. The trial was being held in the historic House of Burgesses in Virginia, where the voices of the patriots had so often thundered forth in times past.

Young Nolan had been accused of plotting against the government and sentence was now to be pronounced. Before doing so the old Colonel asked the prisoner if he had anything to say concerning his plot against the government.

In the stillness of the room the youth arose to fling back these tragic words: "Damn the United States. I wish I may never hear the words 'United States' again."

For a moment every member in that room was struck speechless. The face of the judge turned deathly pale. Each juror looked strained and grim. Half of those men had risked their lives a score of times for the flag and for the nation which this youth cursed so thoughtlessly. Such an insult could not be passed by lightly.

Judge Morgan rose from his place and went to his private room. In fifteen minutes he returned and spoke these words to young Nolan:

"Prisoner, hear the sentence of this court. The court decides, subject to the approval of the President, that you never hear the name of the United States."

Nolan laughed. It seemed to him at that moment that it would make little difference

THOSE WHO LOVE THE FLAG

whether or not he ever heard pronounced the name of his country again.

The judge continued: "Mr. Marshal, take the prisoner to New Orleans in an armed boat and deliver him to the naval commander there, and," continued the judge, slowly, "see that no one mentions the name of the United States to the prisoner while he is on shipboard. Make my respects to Lieutenant Mitchell at New Orleans and give him the same orders. You will receive a written statement from the officer on duty here this evening. The court is dismissed without delay." Thus began the fifty years of exile for *"The Man Without a Country."*

And who was this youth who had so little concern for his country? Philip Nolan was a dashing young officer in the "Legion of the West." When Aaron Burr made his trip down to New Orleans in 1805, Nolan came in contact with him and was charmed by him. Burr plotted to make himself king in this southwest territory and enlisted Nolan in the plot. Later the plans were discovered. The men high in office who were the guilty ones were able to escape justice. Poor Nolan was caught in the mesh. His sentence in the House of Virginia at the hands of Judge Morgan came as the conclusion of this unfortunate affair.

Nolan was first placed on board the ship Intrepid. He was kindly received by the men who talked with him on every conceivable subject. But never once, for years at a stretch, did he hear the name of the United States mentioned. He received foreign papers which had been looked over. He received books that were safe. The clothes he wore were those of an officer, but the gold buttons were removed because they bore the seal of his country.

Years came and went. If the ship on which he sailed was ordered home, he was placed on another, outward bound. Thus was Nolan kept at sea.

The man seemed to bear his punishment bravely. However, all men on board knew that he suffered at heart. On one occasion the men were reading on deck. The book was Scott's *Lay of the Last Minstrel* and Nolan was reading when he came to the lines—

> "Breathes there a man with soul so dead,
> Who never to himself hath said—"

A pained look came over the face of the reader but he plunged on

> "This is my own, my native land.
> Whose heart hath ne'er within him burned
> As home his footsteps he hath turned."

Here Nolan choked and could read no farther. He started up, flung the book overboard, and was not seen outside his stateroom again for two months.

On another occasion his companions had a chance to see how much he loved the country he had cursed. The good ship was far down in the South Seas when they captured a schooner full

THOSE WHO LOVE THE FLAG

of slaves. No one of the sailors could understand their language. Some one suggested Nolan and he was called.

The commanding officer, Vaughn, told Nolan to tell them that they were free. There were wild yells of delight as these dusky natives heard the words. But now they began to cry: "Take us home. Take us to our own country, to our piccaninies and our own women. Take us to our own country. Take us back to our land once more."

At this point Nolan could translate no more. He excused himself and went to his room. Speaking to the young officer with him, he said: "Youngster, let that show you what it is to be without a family, without a home, without a country. And if you are ever tempted to say a word or do a thing that shall put a bar between you and your family, your home, or our country, pray God in his mercy to take you that instant home to his heaven. And for your country, boy, for your flag . . . never dream a dream but of serving as she bids you, though the service carries you through a thousand hells. Remember, boy, that behind all these men you have to do with, behind officers and government, and people even, there is the Country herself, your country . . . and that you belong to her as you belong to your own mother . . ."

From this time on Nolan weakened rapidly. He kept to his room more and spoke less often to the other men. Finally he became so weak that he could not leave his berth. Then one clear day in autumn *The Man Without a Country* was released from his exile.

The Bible of the dead man lay open when they found him and this text was marked:

They desire a country, even a heavenly; wherefore God is not ashamed to be called their God; for he hath prepared for them a city.

On a slip of paper they found written these words:

Bury me at sea; it has been my home, and I love it. But will not someone set up a stone for my memory at Fort Adams or at Orleans, that my disgrace may not be more than I ought to bear? Say on it:

"IN MEMORY OF

PHILIP NOLAN

LIEUTENANT IN THE ARMY OF THE UNITED STATES

He loved his country as no other man loved her; but no man deserved less at her hands."

"What a fine book," said Phil's mother as he concluded the story. "How did Mr. Tucker happen to give it to you?"

"I spoke slightingly of the flag yesterday as it passed by," said Phil, with downcast looks. "Mother, from now on I hope to love and respect our flag as much as Mr. Tucker does."

"That is a worthy resolve, my son, and I hope you keep it," concluded his mother.

(Based on the story, *Man Without a Country*, by Edward E. Hale.)